WHY OLYMPICS AREN'T GOOD FOR US, AND HOW THEY CAN BE

WHY THE OLYMPICS AREN'T GOOD FOR US, AND HOW THEY CAN BE

MARK PERRYMAN

OR Books
New York • London

© 2012 Mark Perryman
Published by OR Books, London and New York.

OR Books is a new type of publishing company that embraces
progressive change in politics, culture and the business of publishing.
We sell our books worldwide, direct to readers. To avoid the waste
of unsold copies, we produce our books only when they are wanted,
either through print-on-demand or as platform-agnostic e-books. Our
approach jettisons the inefficiencies of conventional publishing to better
serve readers, writers and the environment. If you would like to find out
more about OR Books please visit our website at **www.orbooks.com**.

First printing 2012.

Library of Congress Cataloging in Publication Data:
A catalog record for this book is available from the Library of Congress

British Library Cataloging in Publication Data:
A catalog record for this book is available from the British Library

ISBN 978-1-935928-83-6 paperback
ISBN 978-1-935928-84-3 e-book

This book is set in the typeface Caslon.
Typeset by Wordstop, Chennai, India.

Printed by BookMobile in the US and CPI Books Ltd in the UK.
The US printed edition of this book comes on Forest Stewardship
Council-certified, 30% recycled paper. The printer, BookMobile, is 100%
wind-powered.

For Edgar, with the hope there will be better
Olympics to come

Contents

Acknowledgements

Garry Whannel's *Blowing the Whistle* and Alan Tomlinson's *Five Ring Circus*, co-edited with Garry, first convinced me as an aspiring Gramscian that sport was something I could not only watch and do with a degree of political legitimacy, but write about too. I am most grateful to you both for your inspiration and to Alan for your continuing support.

Alan and his co-editor John Sugden must also both be thanked for pestering me to write a chapter for their book *Watching the Olympics*. I was in South Africa for World Cup 2010, looking forward to writing a book on England's trophy-winning campaign. In the event I had plenty of spare time to write their chapter instead, and this more than anything convinced me to write a book of my own on the Olympics. Thanks.

It was after reading Garry's and Alan's books that I wrote my first article on the politics of sport, on the jogging boom and the London Marathon, for *Marxism Today*. Martin Jacques was the kind of editor to take a risk with an unproven writer

and subject. Many thanks Martin. More recently thanks to
Philip Oltermann on Comment is Free at the *Guardian*, Comment Editor on *The Times* Anne Spackman, Greg Leedham
on the *Morning Star* sports desk, Jonathan Rutherford of the
journal *Soundings*, Andy Newman at *www.socialistunity.com*
and Mel Gomes of the blog *The Substantive* for providing me
with the space to write on various sporting themes over the
recent period, articles that have helped me formulate some of
the ideas which now appear in this book.

Students on the Sport and Leisure Management, Sport
Studies and Sport Journalism degrees at the University of
Brighton have listened with sufficient interest to my lectures
on the Olympics to convince me I have something worthwhile
to say. Tim Vyner, Rupert Bassett and the final year Graphic
Comunication class at Bath Spa University also provided an
audience for my ideas on reforming Olympism. The fact you
laughed at my jokes gave me further encouragement to write.

George Galloway, Kevin Ovenden, Rob Hoveman and
Tower Hamlets' Respect Party gathered an impressive crowd
of local activists in the basement of George's then-constituency
office to listen to my impassioned argument that the Olympics
that would take place on the edge of their borough mattered
politically. The enthusiastic response to my presentation was
another further factor in my deciding to write. Thanks again.

Brighton University students Ollie Miller and Tom Glenn

carried out research projects under my supervision on race and the local impact of the Olympics, which also featured at this evening in Tower Hamlets. Your youthful appetite for the investigation, even though you might not have known it at the time, would inspire me to find the energy and commitment to write myself.

Thanks to Colin Robinson of OR Books, with whom I expected to discuss the dual crisis of global capitalism and Liverpool FC, but who ended up convincing me I could write a book on the Olympics in an unfeasibly short time. Colin and his colleague Alex Nunns have provided invaluable editing advice, which has turned this book into something immeasurably better than the one I would have written without their help.

Various earlier versions of this book never went much beyond the planning stage. For showing enough faith in the idea to persuade me to eventually write a book I am grateful to Tariq Goddard of Zero Books, Sally Davison of Lawrence & Wishart and Neal Lawson of the campaign group Compass. Sorry I couldn't deliver for any of you but I hope you nevertheless like what I've ended up writing.

The business I co-founded, Philosophy Football, apart from selling more than a few T-shirts, continues to provide all sorts of ideas of how sport could be reorganized on an ethical and democratic basis. An invaluable experience. Thanks to my co-founder Hugh Tisdale for being generous enough to allow me the time to write alongside my responsibilities to the company.

My main involvement in sport over the past sixteen years has been via the LondonEnglandFans group and the fan-friendly activities we are part of organizing wherever the England football team play abroad. Being involved in a fan-led movement that is both proudly for England and at the same time immersed in the popular internationalism that a Euro or World Cup campaign at its best is has taught me plenty about the potential of sport to unite, as well as divide.

My partner Anne has lived with this book's sometimes painful evolution from idea to research, via writer's block, loss of faith in the project and eventual acceleration to completion. Thanks for the enduring patience. Our three-year-old son Edgar meanwhile has, through his swimming lessons, hurtling around the skateboard park on his scooter, and kicking of a football with wild abandon, successfully warded off any loss of faith in sport's ability to give endless pleasure and sometimes pain.

Finally, thanks to a place, not a person or persons. The South Downs, just above the village of Kingston in East Sussex. A devilishly steep climb to run up, with wild ponies grazing at the side of the stony track. Running along the ridge as I completed this book has convinced me that whatever the corporations, bureaucrats and politicians might do to ruin our enjoyment of

London 2012, the simple appeal of sport can never be extinguished. For that I will always be grateful even if any dreams of winning a medal, of any description, are now long gone.

Ever Fallen in Love With

–something you shouldn't have fallen in love with, to misquote the late 1970s punk band The Buzzcocks. This is not an anti-Olympics book, nor is it against sport. Rather it is about the process that has changed the Olympics into what they have become: a Games that is commercialized and commodified and built on promises that are almost never fulfilled to aid regeneration, boost participation in sport and leave a legacy of well-used facilities. This is not a process that is irreversible and if the Games were organized on a different basis, which I outline, many of those broken promises could instead be kept.

Why the Olympics Aren't Good for Us concentrates mainly on the Summer Olympics (rather than the Winter Games or the Paralympics) since Los Angeles 1984. That's not because the Games before them don't matter. They do. The best book I read in the course of researching this one was Rome 1960: *The Olympics That Changed the World,* by David Maraniss, about an Olympics caught in the midst of the Cold War and the rising civil rights movement led by Martin Luther King Jr. in the USA. But it is after 1984 that the rise and rise of global corporate power has shaped the Games to its own ends, seeking to make the commercialization and commodification of sport something which is universal and to which there is no alternative. My argument is that there is an alternative that would create a better Olympics for all.

It is also not the case that before 1984 the Olympics were perfect, and I don't seek to suggest that they were. The first few Games of the modern era, which started with the Athens Olympics of 1896, excluded women, and racial discrimination was widespread, with many black athletes treated as second-class sporting citizens. Though I refer to and occasionally detail this history, the main focus here is on the post-1984 model of Olympism and how it has defined London 2012.

The first Olympics I fell in love with was the Munich Games of 1972, when I was thirteen years old. These Games became notorious when a group of Israeli athletes was taken hostage by the Palestinian Black September group and ultimately all lost their lives. But any fears of such a deadly act were far from my mind as the Games approached. Instead I concentrated on pestering my parents to fill up at Esso garages so I could complete my Olympic History Sticker Album with the packs that were given away with every four gallons of petrol.

Thirty years later I found myself spending a night at the house of my elder sister, Penelope; we stayed up into the early hours cheering Rhona Martin and her team to Gold in the curling event at the 2002 Winter Olympics. There are, I suspect, many like me, who can measure out their lives in the four-yearly cycle of the Games, each with its never-to-be-forgotten moments, many meaning something even more because of the people we shared them with. For us, the Games have always mattered profoundly. But that doesn't mean we can't hope for a better Games too.

On the day that London won the bid to host the 2012 Games I was busy demonstrating against the G8 summit at Gleneagles, Scotland. My sister phoned me with the news, fully expecting me to be deliriously excited. But I wasn't. For me, the Games had come to represent promises made, then broken. They had become an event that grew from big to bigger to biggest, but to no better end – just a constant round of sport selling itself short to the highest bidder. I had come to realize that the Olympics I once fell in love with weren't what they seemed. After I put my mobile phone back in my pocket I realized I'd like to write a book about how this happened and what could be done about it. I knew there wouldn't be another Olympics in Britain in my lifetime. This was my only chance.

As a writer on sport I've concentrated almost exclusively on football, and in particular what it means to be an England fan.

I've made a bit of a name for myself as a media commentator on the subject. Though I've watched lots of the Olympics on television my only first-hand contact with the Games has come from watching the England football team play in former Olympic stadiums, including the fondly remembered thrashing of Germany 5–1 in the Munich *Olympiastadion*, surrounded by what remained of the Olympic Park from the 1972 Games.

So this is a new topic for me. I begin by discussing a misconception that I believe it is essential to overcome if we are to understand what's happened to the Olympics: the idea that politics has no place in sport. I argue that, far from pursuing the hopeless task of keeping politics out of sport, we should recognize that sport itself is political. Gender, race and class are as much a part of sport as they are of society, in the playing, the governance and the media portrayal of the games we love. Corporate power, sponsors and hugely wealthy individuals dominate sport and affect how we consume it. Domestic and international competitions provide a popular platform for national identity. Sport is political; it is economic; it is cultural. None of this should distort our enjoyment of sport, but we must recognize it.

My academic background is in political science, although latterly I have combined my interest in this area with some work in the field of cultural studies. I draw on both disciplines to explain the way the Olympics has become a 'mega-event', a spectacle in which maintaining the hugeness has become everything, to the detriment of the original purpose of the Olympic Movement. Size is defined by the enormity of the budget, the new builds and the TV audience, not by the actual impact that the Games have.

I haven't written this book to bury the Olympics. Rather I want to revive them. To this end I propose Five New Rings, each a practical organizing principle to reinvent and reimagine the Games. Each ring is linked to the others to produce an Olympics that looks completely different from London 2012. I've written this section of the book with the intent of provoking a discussion that can produce change. Be warned: you will encounter serious suggestions on my part for darts to become an Olympic sport, for Cardiff's Millennium Stadium to host the show jumping final, and for a free-to-watch open-water swimming race to be held in Loch Ness.

Each time I give a talk on the Olympics I set myself the challenge of opening the newspaper that day and finding a London 2012 story to illustrate my critique and justify my alternative. Last December I gave a talk called 'Framing the Olympic Dogma' to third-year Sports Journalism students at the University of Brighton. A splash on the sports pages that morning did just the job. The sports minister, Hugh Robertson, was reported as justifying an additional £40 million that had been allocated to the Olympic opening and closing ceremonies.

'It's about capturing a great national moment for economic advantage. If you talk to the Australians they will tell you they generated many millions of pounds worth of revenue from tourism alone as a result of the Sydney Olympics and that is largely captured in the ceremonies.' I pointed out the emptiness of these claims to my students, referring them to reports from the Australian tourist organizations that revealed not a scrap of evidence for any such uplift resulting from the fireworks and fancy dance routines staged in Sydney. I asked them to think about whether they themselves would choose to visit London because a stadium was being lit up for an evening with a show, however spectacular. I told them it was such mythmaking that had made me question whether I should have fallen in love with the Olympics in the first place. In the end, the fact that another Olympics can be imagined, in the ways that I try to set out in what follows, persuades me that I was right to do so and deepens and cements my belief in the sport of the possible.

From the moment my sister called me with the news that London's bid had won I was highly doubtful that these Olympics would do much good for the country's physical or economic health. My scepticism turned out to be well-founded. Lurid reports of overspending, potential transport chaos and preferential treatment for corporate sponsors have been pretty much daily fare. Some would say this shows that my love for the Olympics is misplaced. But that's why I have written this book: it's not the Olympics that are at fault, it's the failure to turn London 2012 into something better, a Games for all, an Olympics with a purpose. The Olympics aren't good for us, in all the ways I will catalogue. But they can be, with all the ideas I offer.

– Mark Perryman, Lewes, May 2012

CHAPTER ONE
How the Games Are Political

The Olympic torch relay is one of the standout events of the buildup to the opening of the Games in London on 27 July. As the torch is carried along the highways and byways of Britain, uniting the nation in an orgy of premature celebration, it is as well to remember that the spectacle was an invention of the Nazis – brought to you by Adolf Hitler, with stage production by Joseph Goebbels. Conceived for the 1936 Berlin Olympics, the torch relay was originally intended to showcase the racial superiority of the Aryan nation as the flame travelled around Europe. The Nazis were neither the first nor the last to use the Olympics as a political platform, but while indignation at such an abuse of sport is entirely correct, it's too easy to marshal this anger to the simplistic demand that politics be kept out of sport. The point of the story is that sport is always political.

Each Olympic Games is indivisible from the political, economic, social and cultural forces that shape it. The Olympics change as the world changes. The modern Olympics have a heritage dating back more than a hundred years. The late nineteenth century was the era in which most sports were codified, rules agreed, league and record tables established and inaugural international contests held. The first Games, held in Athens in 1896, was part of this process. The Olympics was an event for patricians, immersed in the cult of the gentleman-amateur, to the exclusion of those without the means to train, travel and compete.

The founder of the modern Olympic Movement, Pierre de Coubertin, successfully barred women from the first Games, although remarkably a female Greek runner, Melpomene, managed to evade the officials to complete the marathon. Despite her obvious stamina it took almost a century before women were officially allowed to run this most Olympian of races, in 1984. The early Games were also a product of the Age of Empire as the great powers competed against each other. There were next to no athletes from Black Africa, the Indian subcontinent or other imperial outposts, with those few who were present forced to compete under the flag of the country that had colonized theirs.

The 1900, 1904 and 1908 Games each suffered in different ways from being not much more than add-ons to world trade fairs and commercial exhibitions. These were early, sorry examples of the collision between sport and business from the first era of globalization, when new modes of transport and communication facilitated the growth of international markets in mass-produced goods. This epoch was shattered by military conflict, which inevitably shaped the Olympics with the exclusion of Germany in 1920 and 1948 after the world wars. Conversely, it was surely no accident that the Games were held in Rome in 1960, Tokyo in 1964 and Munich in 1972 – all cities of the defeated Axis powers brought in from their post-war isolation through sport.

With the end of formal empires the second half of the twentieth century was dominated by the Cold War. The Communist Soviet Union and People's Republic of China joined the Olympics for the 1952 Games, sending an important signal of their need to both engage with and compete against the rest of the world, although the Chinese didn't enter another team until 1984. Both countries used the Olympic medals table to boost morale at home and to demonstrate the supposed superiority of their social systems.

The sixties saw the emergence of social movements centred on gender, race and sexuality, each posing new challenges for the Olympic organizers, which they met painfully slowly. A further test came in the form of international terrorism at Munich in 1972, when Israeli athletes were taken hostage by the Palestinian Black September group, ending in lethal carnage. The resulting popular outrage and fear legitimized the security operations that have surrounded the Games ever since.

The end of the Soviet model of state socialism in the late 1980s left only one ideology standing: neo-liberalism, with its winner-takes-all ethos. The race towards marketization and deregulation allowed corporate power to operate on a global scale. This second wave of globalization was expressed in the triumph of the free market, everywhere – even in Communist China, which hosted the most extravagant Games in 2008. But the global financial system proved to be unsustainable and out of control; the resulting crash, recession and debt now form the backdrop to London 2012.

In many ways the current era in Olympic history began at the Los Angeles Games in 1984. Four years previously the USA had failed to persuade most of the world to join it in boycotting the 1980 Moscow Games (the USSR had only recently invaded Afghanistan – for some parts of the world nothing changes but the name of the occupiers). Prior to that in 1976 the Montreal Games had been a huge loss-making commercial disaster for the city, and 1972's Munich Games had been marked by terrorism. Something had to change if the Olympics were to survive. The early 1980s was the era of Reaganomics, and California was US President Reagan's home state. What better place than Los Angeles to put the stamp of corporate America on the Five Rings and transform a symbol that was fast becoming damaged goods?

This was the first Games where the profit motive was

paramount. Sponsorship, endorsement and product-placement deals were all signed with the global multinationals. Coca-Cola, McDonald's and Mars Bar were the kind of brands that could provide the huge sums demanded. For such global products the Olympics provided the perfect promotional platform. This commodification of the Games inevitably had an impact on the athletes too. They demanded, with some degree of justification, that as their sporting efforts now sustained a highly profitable enterprise for a self-perpetuating International Olympic Committee (IOC), they should have a share of the spoils. In 1986, two years after Los Angeles, the strict Olympian code of amateurism was summarily abandoned. Henceforth all profes-sional sportsmen and women would be allowed to compete, creating a professionalization of elite sport across almost every Olympic discipline worldwide. Both processes, commercializa-tion of the Games and professionalization of the athletes, have been key to the dramatic transformation of the Olympics into what they are today.

With huge pressures now being brought to bear on the star athletes to perform it is perhaps no surprise that the next Olympics, Seoul, 1988 are mostly remembered for drugs. The men's 100 metres is the most high profile event of any Games, with the winner dubbed 'the fastest man in the world'. The Seoul race will live in infamy long after the rest of the 1988 Olympics is forgotten. The winner, Ben Johnson, a Canadian sprinting superstar, was disqualified for using performance-enhancing drugs. This wasn't the first case of a drug cheat being caught at the Olympics, but previous incidents had been limited to disciplines that are rarely centre stage, such as weightlifting and athletics field events. The Polish discus thrower Danuta Rosani was the first athlete to be disqualified from the Olympics for drug abuse, at Montreal in 1976, but precious few noticed. The outstanding success of Finnish middle-distance runners in the mid to late 1970s sparked louder mutterings of concern, with rumours of blood-doping to boost their endurance and recovery. Russian and East European athletes and swimmers, particularly sportswomen who looked and sounded somewhat masculine, received a lot of attention, raising Cold War suspicions of Communist cunning.

But when Ben Johnson was caught the impact of the drugs issue transformed the way Olympic sport was viewed, for the worse. His Gold was passed to Carl Lewis, who years later admitted to having tested positive for three banned substances, including prior to the 1988 Games. Despite this serial offending he was never banned by the United States Olympic Committee, who instead hushed up the failed tests. Johnson's exclusion also promoted Linford Christie from Bronze to Silver. Earlier, following a 100-metre heat, Christie had tested positive for a banned substance. A panel at the subsequent hearing decided by a majority of one to give Christie the benefit of the doubt, putting the result down drinking too much ginseng tea. At a small-scale athletics competition eleven years on from Seoul, after coming out of retirement to race, Linford tested positive once again, and this time the British Olympic Association did ban him for life as an athlete and a Team GB–accredited coach. Of the 1988 Gold, Silver and Bronze medal winners in the 100 metres, all were either convicted as charged or continue to have the whiff of suspicion around their athletic careers. This isn't what Olympic sport is supposed to be about.

Barcelona 1992 is the Games invariably put forward as the success story to ward off critics who doubt the value of hosting the Olympics in their city. The claim often made by Barcelona's enthusiasts, mainly from outside Spain, is that the Games unified a country that at the time was only beginning to grapple with the painful legacy of the Franco era. But the truth is different. Barcelona is the capital of Catalonia, a region of Spain that prefers to think of itself as a nation. To add insult to Spanish injury, Madrid is one of the few major European capital cities yet to host the Olympics. Of course Spain's string of Gold medals in 1992 was celebrated right across the country, but the successful hosting of the Games in Barcelona did nothing to reduce support for Catalonian independence; in fact looking at the popularity of the various Catalan political parties twenty years on there is a good case to be made that hosting the Games might have boosted their support. Barcelona

1992 helped reinforce a majoritarian Catalan civic nationalism that has established Catalonia as an autonomous region, with almost all the trappings of a nation state and certainly a very strong sense of its national self. Sport can unite, but not necessarily in the ways intended.

The next Games four years later marked the centenary of the first Olympics of the modern era, at Athens in 1896. The logical host one hundred years on would have been Athens again. Many believe the reason the city had to wait a further eight years for the privilege can be summed up in two words: Coca-Cola. The fizzy drink is one of the grandly titled 'Worldwide Olympic Partners'. I know this because it's printed on every can of Diet Coke that I knock back. And where is Coca-Cola's headquarters? Atlanta. Amongst those who shared the sense of surprise at Atlanta's victory over Athens, many felt this had been a major factor in deciding which city should host the centenary Olympics. What is certain is that these were the first Games where the intrusion of unsavoury business practices into the IOC bidding process attracted sufficient public attention for the Olympic Movement to at least take some notice. It is an association the IOC has been forced to live with ever since.

Sport, unlike almost any other cultural form, can hurdle barriers of culture, language or politics, giving it an unrivalled position as a means of promoting goods to a global audience.

The process that began in Los Angeles in 1984 deepened in Atlanta in 1996, with the corporatization of the Olympics becoming a defining characteristic as sponsors established themselves as one of the most powerful components of an Olympic Games. Staging the 1996 event in Atlanta was in large measure a recognition of this accelerating phenomenon.

Sydney in 2000 offers perhaps a more cheerful picture-postcard Olympic memory. A sporting moment can some-times crystallize social or political changes within a nation. As Cathy Freeman, the Australian Aboriginal sprinter, streaked around the track to win the 400-metre Gold medal, kitted out in an all-in-one skintight green-and-Gold Lycra suit complete with hood, she was chased every inch of the way by the light of thousands of camera phones flashes capturing her moment of glory. This was more than an instant of supreme sporting achievement. For Australia's Aboriginal community it repre-sented both recognition from the majority white population and acceptance, however temporary it ultimately proved to be. Inequality, discrimination, racism and disputes over land rights didn't disappear just because Cathy was a national heroine. Her success was the exception, not the rule, but for a moment it pointed to a different version of Australia.

Greece today symbolizes the Eurozone in crisis: a country in catastrophic debt with a population facing unimaginable levels of austerity for decades to come. But before the financial

meltdown hit the Greek economy the dereliction and disrepair of virtually all the 2004 venues demonstrated the failure
of the Olympics to provide the promised regeneration to the
city. Almost every Games of the past three decades has been
accompanied by the claim that it would give a boost to investment, infrastructure and tourism, and in almost every case the
prospectus has been false. But in Athens the failure could not
have been starker as the Olympic legacy crumbled against a
backdrop of out-of-control Greek national debt, caused largely
by the 2008 international banking crisis.

The year of the financial collapse was also the year of the
Beijing Olympics, and once again the political message of the
Torch relay was in the spotlight. On a London High Street in
April 2008, during the buildup to the Games, the diminutive
five-foot-nothing former BBC TV children's show Blue Peter
presenter Konnie Huq was almost knocked to the ground by
a protester as she completed her stretch of Torch carrying.
Those protesting wanted a boycott of the Beijing Olympics
over China's invasion and mistreatment of Tibet. Stopping
the torch in its tracks was a highly effective way of getting
this message across, and it was not an isolated incident. The
worldwide opposition to the 2008 Torch relay was so huge that
leg after leg had to be either scrapped or policed so heavily that
the Torch was removed from view. For this year's Games the
London 2012 organizers mindful of similar protests possibly

sparked by Britain's role in Afghanistan or Iraq, decided to drop the international part of the relay entirely and keep proceedings to good old Blighty alone.

All of this should be enough to establish a common-sense understanding that the Olympics have always been political. The greatness of the achievement of being faster and stronger than anyone else has forever been accompanied and occasionally obscured by the social, economic and political context. Few would seriously suggest that Beijing 2008 wasn't as much about providing a global media platform to entrench China's position as a world superpower as it was about the events in and around the Bird's Nest stadium.

Yet the mantra of much of the sporting establishment in the 1970s and 1980s persists: sport and politics are separate. Today South Africa is home to the world's most revered elder statesman, Nelson Mandela. It is a rainbow nation, which under African National Congress governments has hosted the football, rugby and cricket World Cups. It is almost certainly only a matter of time before it hosts the Olympics too. But in the 1970s Mandela was imprisoned on Robben Island and Soweto wasn't a stop on the tourist trail but a place where school kids would be shot dead if they demonstrated for the right to be taught in their own language. And sport? If you were black you would automatically be barred from representing your country, whatever your talent and ability.

'No sport with an abnormal society' was the philosophy of the protests and those who campaigned for a boycott of any sporting contact with Apartheid South Africa, including their team's expulsion from the Olympics. 'Keep politics out of sport' came the retort. This was one of the sharpest divisions ever seen in international sport. But the force of the argument won through: if nation's political system denied an athlete the right to run, play or compete for his or her nation simply because of their skin colour then playing sport with that nation could no longer persist.

The ferocity of the pro- and anti-apartheid arguments seems almost a world away now. But what they helped to reveal was how sport can never fail to be shaped by the society in which it is played. Nobody can keep politics out of sport, however hard they try, because sport is political. Grasp this and we can begin to understand the processes by which the Olympics has turned into what it has become, but also how they could yet be transformed into something better. Let the Games begin.

CHAPTER TWO
The Promise of London 2012 and Why It Won't Be Kept

On Saturday 2 July 2005, just four days before London was awarded the 2012 Olympic Games, the Live8 concert took place in Hyde Park. A huge open-air gig, it was the culmination of a campaign to pressure a gathering of the G8 leaders, being hosted by Tony Blair and meeting just outside Edinburgh, to cancel Third World Debt. Begun by NGOs and aid charities the movement was eventually fronted by Live Aid veterans Bono and 'Sir' Bob Geldof. On the outer fringes of the campaign was a post–Seattle and Genoa anti-capitalist movement committed to direct action. All were united, to the extent a coalition of this diversity was ever going to be, behind the message 'Make Poverty History', worn on discreet white plastic wristbands.

Bono joined another 'Sir', Paul McCartney, to open the show with their version of 'Sergeant Pepper's Lonely Hearts Club

Band'. The concert, broadcast on primetime BBC TV, came complete with scruff-free mosh pit at the front of the stage where the great and the good could set out their deckchairs.

One of the stars of the show, Coldplay frontman Chris Martin, in a not-uncharacteristic statement of rock-and-roll self-aggrandizement, declared from the stage that Live8 was 'the greatest thing that's ever been organized, probably in the history of the world.'

In 2001 hundreds of thousands of mainly Italian demonstrators had almost brought the G8 meeting in Genoa to a stop. In the face of the most brutal policing seen in Europe for years, one protester was shot dead and many suffered serious head injuries after the baton charges. In 1999 when a similar convention of global leaders, the World Trade Organization, met in Seattle the tens of thousands who marched managed to halt the proceedings. Neither depended on a pop concert to mobilize, nor needed Bono, Geldof, Coldplay and a supporting cast to inspire their resistance, which rapidly became global.

Live8 of course did reach a far bigger audience than those likely to demonstrate, commit acts of non-violent direct action, or mount blockades. That's a worthwhile achievement in itself, many would argue. But critics, in increasing numbers, have also come to question whether these kinds of mega-events are ever more obsessed with simple size, at the expense of their message. Celebrity rhetoric, repeated by politicians grateful for

the stardust accompanying it, replaces the less glamorous reality of social movements for change. The mega-event becomes
a means to its own end, often divorced from its original sentiments. It was significant, therefore, that in the week that began
with Live8, London was selected as host city for the 2012
Olympics.

London had been on the International Olympics Committee
(IOC) shortlist since the previous year. Following an exhaus-
tive vetting process the British capital was up against Paris,
Madrid, Moscow and New York. For the 1996 and 2000
Games Manchester had been considered a plausible enough
venue to be allowed to bid on Great Britain's behalf, as had
Birmingham in 1992. But despite Barcelona proving itself a
more than passable host in 1992, and to a lesser extent Atlanta
in 1996, the shift ever since the 2000s has been for the host
cities to be capitals of their respective countries (or, in the
case of Sydney, a city that can trip you up in Trivial Pursuit
by being the capital in all but constitutional name). Former
Olympic cities such as Los Angeles, Munich and Melbourne
are not exactly backwaters in their respective countries, but the
prestige-obsession of the IOC meant their like would probably
never again be serious contenders to host the Games.

Manchester, despite hosting the Commonwealth Games as
recently as 2002, was impolitely told by the British government
to forget about pitching for 2012. Thus right from the start an

imbalance was established by the London bid: every decision would be moulded to suit the IOC's interests.

In the final vote Paris was the favourite right to the last, and with good reason. In 1998 France had hosted the football World Cup, with the final in Paris at the brand new *Stade de France* stadium. The Stade de France is located in St Denis, part of the Parisian 'red belt' of deprived, working-class and multicultural communities; it would have been perfect for a Games that today are supposedly as much about the transformation and regeneration of the neighbourhoods where they are held as Gold medal–winning performances.

In 2003 the same stadium was the venue for the World Athletics Championship. Unlike the new Wembley, the stadium authorities in France had the good sense to find a way to lay an athletics track beneath the football pitch, ready to be used for what is football's third biggest global sporting event after the World Cup and the Olympics. With retractable front row seats this was a neat and cost-effective way of producing a world-class multi-use stadium.

London, on the other hand, had never hosted the World Athletics Championship and England's 1966 World Cup was back in the days when just 16 countries participated, not the 32 of today, with virtually no travelling fans, compared to the hundreds of thousands who now attend.

The London bid's final presentation was introduced by

HRH Princess Anne, with contributions from Sebastian Coe, Prime Minister Tony Blair, Ken Livingstone and others. It was a stellar lineup: a royal who had also competed at the Olympics (Montreal 1976, in the three-day-event horse trials); an Olympian who had won multiple Gold medals; one of the world's most famous statesmen; and London's popular mayor.

Princess Anne opened the proceedings, extending best wishes via letter from her mother, the Queen, to the assembled delegates. 'I have been impressed by the way everyone has united behind London's bid. As a country, we share a passion for sport,' the Queen's message read. In light of reports at the time of falling levels of participation in physical activity and a resultant obesity epidemic, it would not have been treasonable, or even unreasonable, to ask what evidence there was for this touted popular unity. Indeed, the government's own Minister of Sport, Richard Caborn, also a member of the 2012 bid team, had previously declared that 'The growing prevalence of obesity across the population is a serious issue which needs to be tackled,' while Belinda Linden of the British Heart Foundation had stated in a well-published survey of the state of the nation's health that 'Inactivity is implicated in over a third of deaths from heart attacks, and worryingly, is on the increase.'

Never mind. The presentation moved on swiftly from the regal pleasantries. Next up was Sebastian Coe who, having ended his athletics career in the mid-eighties, had gone on to be elected as a Tory MP for the Cornish constituency of Falmouth and Camborne. Less successful in his new vocation, he served only one term before being rejected by the voters in the New Labour landslide of 1997. Following the well-trodden path of politicians favoured by their party's higher-ups but unable to muster votes, he took his place as Lord Coe in the unelected House of Lords in 2000. But none of this would matter here. His credibility in any gathering of Olympic dignitaries could not be challenged. In their impressionable midst Coe was that rare thing: a living legend. He stirred their hearts with a rousing tale of how London would 'reach young people all around the world … [and] connect them with the inspirational power of the Games…so they are inspired to choose sport.'

Coe was followed by a politician who, as socialist leader of the Greater London Council (GLC) in an earlier era, might have been Coe's worst nightmare. But the firebrand previously known as 'Red Ken' was now older and cuddlier, his sharp edges smoothed by the responsibilities of mayoral office. It was Livingstone who made the connection with Live8. Recalling the previous weekend's concert in Hyde Park he declared, 'If you want to mobilise the youth of the world, start in London.' What underpinned the parallel being drawn here remained unclear but it seemed to go down well enough with the assembled delegates. As London mayor Livingstone had previously shown little or no interest in sport in the capital; now his enthusiastic support for the Games was informed by his belief that they would deliver for East London much needed economic renewal. He dubbed London 2012 'The Regeneration Games.'

The final star member of the presentation team was Prime Minister Tony Blair, who emphasized the unanimous backing London 2012 had secured. 'My entire Government and the main opposition parties are united behind the bid. It has total political support.' In claiming this, Blair was clearly right. Virtually unconditional support for the Olympics was present from the start across the political spectrum. When Livingstone was defeated by Conservative Boris Johnson in the 2008 London mayoral election, the unconditional enthusiasm for the Games flowed seamlessly from one mayor to another. Likewise two years later, in 2010 when the Labour government was replaced by the Con-Dem coalition, Cameron and Clegg were as supportive of the Games as Blair's successor, Gordon Brown, had been. Whether this airtight bubble of consensus extended beyond Westminster to the country as a whole was a question that went almost entirely unasked by the London-based commentariat.

The promise of how London and the country would benefit from the Olympics hardly seemed to merit a murmur of a challenge. But in fact substantial question marks can be placed against each element of this three-part promise: first, that the

Olympics would massively increase participation in sport, particularly amongst young people; second, that the Games would significantly boost economic regeneration; third, that the host city's image would be transformed for the better, attracting tourists who wouldn't otherwise have visited.

Will hosting the Olympics boost participation in sport? Investigative journalist David Conn examined the evidence and reported in the *Guardian* newspaper: 'No previous Olympic Games or other major tournament has ever led directly to an increase in people taking part in sport. If anything the opposite seems to happen. Sport England research has shown that ordinary mortals watching, from their sofas, "models of perfection" performing on the elite stage can actually be put off trying to do more exercise.'

There appears to be little correlation between hosting major sporting events, or achieving success in them, and popular levels of participation in sport. Take the case of Finland. An estimated 55% of Finns exercise three times a week compared to only 21% of Britons. The country can boast being among the healthiest in Europe. Yet Finland last hosted the Olympics in 1952, and the most recent global sporting event that took place there was the inaugural World Athletics Championship in 1983. At the Beijing Olympics the country finished a lowly 44th in the medals table. Finland's position as the healthiest nation in the developed world is related to factors that have little to do with high profile sports jamborees, as Mika Pykko, executive director of the Finnish Centre for Health Promotion, explained to David Conn: 'We are a more equal society. We have a high level of education and generally, educated people exercise more. We still have a challenge but historically have always been close to nature and so the culture of walking is still there.'

Or look at Australia, often seen as Team GB's closest rival when it comes to Olympic medals. A report commissioned by the Australian government after the country finished a disappointing sixth to GB's fourth in the Beijing medal table suggested that the massive skewing of sport investment to elite-level competition such as the Olympics might be misplaced:

> Evidence shows that participation in physical activity is dominated by non-organised sport and physical recreation. Moreover, this is an increasing trend: aerobics and fitness activities were the biggest growth areas for participation between 2001 and 2008.
>
> The growth of time-poor two-income families leaves little time for sport. As a consequence, exercise is 'purchased' and 'fitted into' a schedule. People are moving towards activities that are able to suit lifestyle and time constraints and thus

provide the most flexible options. Seven out of the ten growth areas in this time span were activities such as walking, running, cycling and aerobics/gym exercise – essentially activities that can be done on an individual basis. Apart from aerobics, in 2008, participation in the five most popular sports in Australia largely took the form of non-organized involvement.

While some traditional sports are growing, there is substantial growth in the number of people engaged in non-structured physical recreational activities – such as skateboarding, skiing, golf, cycling and more informally organised competitions such as mixed indoor cricket, netball and volleyball.

The report provoked a furious response by Australia's sporting establishment, which sought to defend the enormous funding provided for elite performers in high-profile Olympic sports. Commenting on the row from afar in the *Observer* journalist Kevin Mitchell noted drily that the report's analysis was being accused of 'putting the general health of the nation over medals.'

If mass participation in sport is an unproven byproduct of the Olympics, what about the idea that the Games could provide stimulus for a depressed part of the host city? The thinking behind this approach was articulated by two of New

Labour's favoured thinktanks, Demos and the Institute for Public Policy Research, in their joint report *After the Gold Rush*. Published as the Olympic bid was being finalized in 2004, the report brought together a collection of contributors to identify the measures needed for a sustainable Olympic legacy. 'The Olympics must be embedded within existing mainstream programmes and policy agendas that start well before 2012 and continue well after,' the report insisted, adding, 'For local communities to fully benefit from any opportunities, there must be an investment in community capacity and ownership.' These sentiments expressed the kind of centrist politics that Blairism had come to represent, and they have been regularly repeated by Labour's Tory successors in office. Hindsight is a wonderful thing, but as the Greek people try to resist a programme of austerity almost unimaginable in its intensity it is salient to recall the introduction to the Demos/IPPR report, written in the afterglow of the Athens Olympics of 2004 by then Olympics minister, Tessa Jowell: 'This summer, we've seen the transforming effect of hosting the Olympics. Athens is a changed place: cleaner, brighter, easier to get around, vibrant and modern. In Athens, as with Barcelona in 1992, the Olympics was a catalyst for investment, and the Games themselves an opportunity to present the city and country in a new light.' Of course Labour MP Jowell couldn't have anticipated the devastating impact on the Greek economy of the global recession that began three years later. But long before the tidal wave of austerity broke, the signs weren't looking good for the Athenian 'new light' of her breathless enthusing.

It's true that the Athens Games refuted many of the more pessimistic prognostications that preceded it. The facilities would never be finished on time, the British media confidently predicted, and the city's infrastructure would never be able to cope. In the end everything was ready and the Games passed off without too many complaints. The air pollution in the city wasn't as bad as feared, although the smog and high daily temperatures didn't favour the endurance events. And of course the historic setting provided a supremely evocative backdrop for Greece's second-only hosting of the Games since their modern reinvention in 1896. But the transformation that Jowell gushed about simply never materialized. The increasingly sorry state of almost all of the former Athens 2004 venues in the wake of the Games has been well-publicized. Twenty-one out of twenty-two of the stadiums, arenas, sports halls and swimming pools built for the Games are either derelict, in a state of disrepair, boarded up or unable to find a buyer and underused. As the Beijing Games opened four years later Athens faced a bill estimated at £500m simply to maintain this ghost town of Olympian extravagance. And, according to research commissioned by the London Assembly, *A Lasting Legacy for London? Assessing the Legacy of the Olympic and Paralympic*

Games, published in 2007, the increase in jobs for the Greek population proved to be remarkably short-term: 'Immediately following the Games, the positive employment effect moved into reverse. In the 3 months after the Games, September–November 2004, Greek industry lost 70,000 jobs, the majority in construction.'

In an attempt to understand what went wrong, academics Evangelia Kasimati and Peter Dawson published a report in 2009 entitled *Assessing the Impact of the 2004 Olympic Games on the Greek Economy.* They pointed out that 'the overwhelming majority of the costs have been financed by the public purse, this appears to reflect the growing importance governments have attached to the notion of Olympic legacy.' They noted that the same applies to London 2012. Worryingly, they concluded that while the immediate impact of the Athens Games was quite positive, 'the long-term economic legacy effects with respect to both GDP and unemployment appear to be quite modest.'

A similar analysis had been undertaken to assess the economic impact of the Sydney Games, held four years earlier. The findings of *The Sydney Olympics, Seven Years On* by James Giesecke and John Madden of Monash University's Centre of Policy Studies were, if anything, even more damning: 'In terms of purely measurable economic variables the Sydney Olympics had a negative effect on New South Wales and Australia as a whole.' According to Giesecke and Madden that doesn't mean Australians weren't willing to support the Sydney Games; rather, the promises made proved impossible to fulfil. 'Taking into account a possibly higher preference for sport by Australians it is feasible that Australians were willing to cover this loss,' they said. 'However it now seems… unlikely that the Games produced a double dividend of intangible benefits and an economic boost of the sort previously thought.'

Previously, in 2000, the International Association of Sport Economists published a paper reviewing the regenerative effects on Atlanta that had occurred as a result of staging the games there in 1996. In *Bidding for the Olympics: Fool's Gold?* Robert Baade and Victor Matheson point out,

> To a significant degree the Olympics represent an alien industry, one that does not connect or mesh well with established businesses. In addition to the Olympic Stadium, ACOG (Atlanta Committee for the Olympic Games) created an International Horse Park of 1,400 acres, spent $17 million on the Wolf Creek Shooting Complex and another $10 million on the Lake Lanier Rowing Center. These facilities may be unique, but explanations are required for how these rather esoteric developments fit with other industries and contribute to

the economies of scale arguments that underlie, at least in part, the sectoral clustering, cumulative causation and disequilibrium dynamic adjustment models that represent contemporary explanations for the rapid growth in some MSAs (Metropolitan Statistical Areas).

While their analysis is rich in economist gobbledygook the authors nevertheless offer a common-sense conclusion that couldn't be clearer. 'Diverting scarce capital and other resources from more productive uses to the Olympics very likely translates into slower rates of economic growth than that which could be realized in the absence of hosting the Olympic Games.'

The defenders of the Olympics invariably endeavour to get round these kinds of short-term cost-benefit imbalances by demanding that critics consider the longer-term positives in the shape of image and attitudinal shifts towards the host city and nation. They claim these will lead to increases in tourism, inward investment and better economic prospects. But for Sydney there was little or no boost of this kind. An Australian Tourism Industry report based on detailed survey evidence, *The Sydney Olympics and Foreign Attitudes to Australia*, by authors that included Nancy Rivenburgh, a former Professor of Olympism at Barcelona's Centre for Olympic Studies, offered an entirely plausible explanation for the crucial American

market's reluctance to see Australia as a newly desirable destination for tourism and investment: 'Given that the Sydney
Olympics were constructed as global entertainment, US
media-coverage of the Games and Australia, for the most part,
simply reinforced the already-held imagery of Australia as a
far-away exotic location peopled by friendly folk who seemed
almost American. Given that there was no Sydney 2000 media
coverage that served to fundamentally challenge already-held
images and attitudes, American perceptions, not surpris-
ingly, remained largely constant before and after the Sydney
Olympics.'

It's actually self-evident that reaching out globally to those
unaware of a host city's potential for business and fun is almost
impossible to achieve in the space of two weeks of hurried TV
shots of Olympian feats in stadia that look pretty much the
same the world over. With only the occasional scenic television backdrop to the main action taking place in the sporting
contests themselves, why should any more profound change in
the perception of the host city occur among the global audience? After watching the action from London 2012 how many
additional tourists in future years are likely to step out beyond
the city's existing major tourist destinations to investigate the
attractions of Tower Hamlets, Newham, Waltham Forest and
Hackney? To ask the question is to answer it.

With the widely acclaimed redevelopment of the city that

accompanied them, the Barcelona Games, held in 1992, can certainly be regarded as an exception to the general dismal pattern. But, two decades on, the factors that accounted for the singular success of the event in the Catalan capital have been conveniently obscured. In a piece they wrote for the travel trade's *Tourism Insights*, website business experts Iris Hillier and Rafael Isun cite four key reasons why matters took a different, more positive course in Barcelona.

First, the Games took place just ten years after Spain's first democratic elections following the death of General Franco. The country had only recently joined the European Union. Though Spain had been a popular holiday destination during the Fascist era, its attraction for tourists significantly increased in the wake of these changes and created a domestic mood of hope and expectation that greatly boosted its potential for hosting the games.

Second, Barcelona had hardly any kind of global profile prior to 1992. Very few of the journalists covering the Games had visited the city previously, and consequently knowledge of the many attractions that Barcelona had to offer was low. The architecture, culture, cosmopolitanism and engagement of the local population could hardly fail to impress.

Third, a few years after the Games took place, European air travel was deregulated and the boom in cheap budget flights began. The overseas city weekend break became a reality for millions, and Barcelona was better placed than most to take advantage of it. With thirty new hotels built, the city had more than doubled the number of available tourist beds in preparation for the Games. Within a year of the Games occupancy levels had fallen from 80% to just 50%. But the arrival of low-cost travel soon took up the slack.

None of these advantages are available to London in 2012. The city is already a world-famous tourist destination; none of its landmarks are likely to be unfamiliar to the global media attending or the global audience following the Games on TV. And any boom in budget airline travel is long past.

One of the best critiques of the Olympic promise comes from the European Tour Operators Association (ETOA). A trade organization for European travel companies, the ETOA is not a hotbed of anti-corporate campaigners or an encounter group for rosy-eyed sports romantics. It's hard to imagine that if there were any evidence that the Games would boost tourism they wouldn't be among the Olympics' biggest cheerleaders. But the ETOA states in its authoritative *Olympic Report* published in 2006: 'The audiences regularly cited for such events as the Olympics are exaggerated. Attendances at the Games displace normal visitors and scare tourists away for some time. There appears to be little evidence of any benefit to tourism of hosting an Olympic Games, and considerable evidence of damage.'

One point is particularly well made. Picking on four of

London's most well-known destinations for football, tennis and cricket they point out that 'Wembley, Wimbledon, St John's Wood and Kennington have not become major non-sporting resorts.' A cursory wander around the streets surrounding Wembley Stadium, the biggest location of the four, would quickly confirm this. Fast-food bars do a decent trade on match days and thus proliferate, pubs take on extra staff, but that's about it. The sort of structural urban renewal which London 2012's supporters promised is almost entirely absent.

The report also comments on the likelihood of global TV coverage further expanding London's reputation as a must-visit destination: 'Sports fans watch television in order to enjoy the sport. This activity is notoriously narrowly focused, as viewers get ever closer to the athletes, and each move is broken down frame by frame. The moment this is over, their attention is drawn to the next event.' The Olympic stadium, pool and velodrome will go down in history as the places where epic contests were fought and Gold medals won. But except for a dedicated few, there will be little desire to visit them subsequently. Instead, within a few months, all eyes will be on Rio de Janeiro, host of the 2016 Games.

The ETOA report suggests that the impact on tourism during an Olympic year for a host city is not much more than negligible; often it's actually negative. In 1996 in Georgia, home state of the host city Atlanta, hotel occupancy rates fell from 73% in the previous year to 68%. Sydney 2000 saw hotel occupancy fall steadily as the Games approached, from 83% in March to 68% in July and August, before a modest recovery to 80% during the Games themselves. In an update of their 2006 report the ETOA established that Beijing in 2008 recorded 30% fewer tourists in July of the Olympic year compared to the same month in 2007, with a 5% decline year-on-year for August when the Games were taking place, and 25% below in the following months through to December. A recovery has since occurred but this is ascribed to Beijing hoteliers slashing room rates rather than the attraction of a visit to the Bird's Nest stadium. The ETOA points to a rarely mentioned consequence of hosting the Olympics: 'Olympic visitors effectively scare other visitors away. Regular tourists assume that congestion and increased prices are a feature of Mega-Events.'

But if overall figures for the year in which the Olympics take place are often down, surely the Games attract greater tourist income whilst they are actually taking place? Not according to the ETOA, whose study shows that the Olympics, when looked at in financial terms, don't deliver. This is due to the nature of the visitors who accompany the holding of the Games: 'During the Olympic period, the entire bed-stock of a destination is devoted to the travelling officials, the press and spectators. These visitors are unlike "regular" tourists, having different spending and behaviour patterns. They are not interested in "tourism" – they are interested in sport. They tend not to spend money on leisure and entertainment, and when not in the stadia they watch events on TV rather than engaging in other activities.'

Any financial benefit from Olympic tourism is almost exclusively short-term and hotel-specific, jacking up the room prices for a few weeks for a clientele who are unlikely ever to visit again, as they move on to the next major sporting event. The ETOA ends up with a withering assessment of the likely benefit of the Games for tourism: 'During the Olympics, a destination effectively closes for normal business. The repercussions are felt before and after: both tourists and the tour operators that supply them are scared off immediately before and during the events. This "absence" then creates its own effect, as the normal conveyor belt of contented customers begetting new arrivals has been broken.'

Although perhaps the most visible, tourism is of course only one of the economic and social benefits the Olympics seek to claim as their own. However, in *Bidding for the Olympics* Baade and Matheson offer the beginnings of an alternative to the existing Olympic system: 'If cities are intent on hosting the Olympic Games they must do the obvious, that is they must take steps to counteract the monopoly power of the International Olympic Committee.' This is precisely what London and every other bidding city has failed to do. The IOC has been allowed to elevate itself into a kind of all-powerful quasi-state, with the affiliated nations of the world, and the contestants in the quadrennial beauty pageant to determine the host city, fully compliant in this development. As Baade and Matheson point out, there is a compelling need to challenge the IOC: 'It is in the collective interest of potential host cities to devise means to change the nature of the bidding process.'

The Games are designed to serve the interests of the IOC in maintaining and defending their very particular model of the Olympics, and not the needs of the host city and nation. As Baade and Matheson conclude, the IOC is rarely if ever concerned to find 'the most effective methods for integrating Olympic infrastructure needs with the present economy and a vision of its future.' The consequence of this is that 'Cities that succeed in hosting the Olympics may well only find fools' Gold for their efforts.' With this as our overview all the complaints of overspending, locations, ticket pricing and post-Games legacy make some kind of sense. The IOC has its version of what it wants the Olympics to look like and any attempt to break with this results in the bid failing. If selected, the host city will have been so successfully incorporated into the IOC's agenda that any ongoing challenge is soon extinguished. Staffed by sports' own political class, in many cases with no obvious constitu-ency of athletes to which they are accountable, the IOC and its local variants, the Olympic Delivery Authority (ODA) and the London Organising Committee of the Olympic and Paralympic Games (LOCOG), trap elected politicians and much of the media in their gaze of unsubstantiated expectation.

It is no accident that this process has occurred over the past thirty years, dating back to the first Games to be driven explicitly by commercial interests: Los Angeles 1984. City economies have experienced a shift from industries of manufacturing and accumulation to service and consumption. This has created a spiralling contest over a city's badge value and identity status, which the Olympics and other mega-events promise, with little or no basis in reality, to enhance.

By unpicking the fallacies of the IOC and its supporters, the entire promise of the Olympics as something socially benevolent is demolished. But more important, a vision for an alternative Olympism can begin to be constructed. However any such clear-sighted critical thinking was pushed to the far margins in the aftermath of the IOC's vote on 6 July 2007 in Singapore. The nation's TV screens, along with every other available media outlet, were splattered with the joyful incredulity that London would host the biggest global sporting event of all.

Twenty-four hours later the celebrations were brought to an abrupt halt by bombs that exploded across the capital's transport network with the kind of death and bloody carnage not seen since the IRA bombing campaign a generation ago.

In the wake of 9/11 many loud voices had expressed distrust

of a Muslim community they had decided was at best in denial over their collective responsibility for the horrific assault on the Twin Towers and at worst guilty by association of faith, race or both. After London's 7/7 this message was amplified, turning into an all-out assault on the case for a multicultural Britain. In the *Daily Telegraph* veteran commentator W.F. Deedes accused post-war Britain of a 'belief in the blessing of a multiracial society, left free to hold whatever allegiances it pleased.' And in a speech that set out what was to become one of the core themes of his short-lived premiership, Labour leader Gordon Brown claimed, 'We are waking from a once-fashionable view of multiculturalism, which, by emphasising the separate and the exclusive, simply pushed communities apart. What was wrong about multiculturalism was not the recognition of diversity but that it over-emphasised separateness at the cost of unity. Continually failing to emphasise what bound us together as a country, multiculturalism became an excuse for justifying separateness, and then separateness became a tolerance of – and all too often a defence of – even greater exclusivity.'

From left and right a caricature of multiculturalism was used as a cover to break with the kind of celebratory diversity that the Olympic bid had seemed, at least for a moment, to repre-sent. In Singapore, as the London bid presentation approached its climactic ending, Seb Coe had welcomed on stage thirty youngsters, 'each from East London, from the communities who will be touched most directly by our Games. Thanks to London's multicultural mix of 200 nations, they also represent the youth of the world … Their families have come from every continent. They practice every religion and every faith.' Was there any box in the table of diversity these children didn't tick? It was a compelling image of London as a global city. Many observers suggested that it was this piece of theatre that gave London the final edge over Paris. Coe had even added a perhaps risky dig at the delegates when he introduced the children with the question, 'Why are so many here, taking the place of businessmen and politicians?' But this was a flimsy populism, a kind of corporate multiculturalism, a presentation of unity through diversity which obscured the realities of representation. Of course sport can act as a popular starting point for a conversation on ethnic and national identity, but if that is the beginning, middle and end of our understanding of racism then the fallout from the events of 7/7 proved soon after that it hadn't taken us very far.

As he paraded the youngsters 'representing' London across the Singapore stage it might have been useful to ask Coe, or even the children themselves, a few questions: What was it like growing up in Tower Hamlets, Newham and Hackney, among the poorest boroughs in the city? What jobs did their parents have, if they had jobs at all? What opportunities in terms of health, education and housing could they look forward to?

How would they and their families be able to afford tickets to watch the Games they were on the stage to promote? Such inquiries would certainly have told us more about the realities of life in contemporary Britain than the shallow photo-opportunity on offer.

Without this kind of careful unpicking of patterns of exclusion and inclusion, sport's symbolism remains precisely that, a symbol incapable of effecting the kind of substantial change which is often claimed on its behalf. And thus Prime Minister Cameron can very publicly embrace the importance of London's global mix in the Olympic bid while declaring, 'we have allowed the weakening of our collective identity. Under the doctrine of state multiculturalism, we have encouraged different cultures to live separate lives, apart from each other and apart from the mainstream.'

The forces of integration and difference reflect a set of power relations and consequential resistance that, like the national identities they help to define, are always in motion. Sport plays an important part in this process, but its role is partial and overhyped at the expense of examining why the black athletes who represent Britain on the pitch, in the ring or on the race track are not replicated in anything like equal numbers in the boardroom, on the front benches or on the committees that run sport's governing bodies. Writer on race and sport Dan Burdsey provides a poignantly powerful observation on how the racialization of sport is often experienced. Apart from the athletes on the track, 'You will often see a significant presence of minority ethnic people in the stadium: they will be directing you to your seat or serving your refreshments. The racialised historical antecedents and continuing legacy, of these roles – entertaining or serving the white folk – should not be lost within the contemporary clamour of positivity.' Experienced in this way, an Olympic Park built at the centre of three of Britain's most multicultural boroughs will expose many of the inclusions and exclusions that persist in our society, or at least it will, if anyone actually notices.

So long as sport is presented as a conveniently accessible symbol of multiculturalism, with the added advantage of increasing our chances of getting on the medal-winning podium, a constructive dialogue on race and national identity has at least the chance of beginning. But it will stop pretty soon after unless the awkward and painful structures of power, which underpin racism, are also addressed. Instead we often fall back on a make-believe 'state-sponsored multiculturalism', which *Guardian* journalist Gary Younge correctly describes as a 'fiction rooted in the fear of what has never been', opposed to a popular multicultural experience of 'fact rooted in considerable achievements of who we have become.' Left isolated from this broader conversation, sport's contribution to meaningful cultural and social change is hugely diminished. The prospect of hosting the Olympics becomes a morale-boosting antidote to the horrors London witnessed on 7/7, but fails to have significant impact on the popular revival of racism those terrible events ignited.

This then was the week that was. Seven days that began with McCartney and Bono opening Live8 with their 2005 version of 'Sergeant Pepper's Lonely Hearts Club Band' ended with terror on London's buses and Tube system and grief that soon translated into a wave of popular self-doubt about the differences that existed between us, on issues of race and faith in particular, and what kind of home truths they held about Britain and its national identity. And, in the middle of all this, complete with its promises of participation, regeneration and image makeover, a set of mistruths framed by the myth-making of mega-event culture and the flimsy symbolism of corporate multiculturalism. London to host the Olympics in 2012? I could hardly wait.

CHAPTER THREE

Five New Olympic Rings

The Olympic Five Rings have no basis in the Ancient Greek version of the Games. Designed by Baron de Coubertin, they were first used at the 1920 Antwerp Games. Instantly and globally recognizable, the five interlocking rings represent the Earth's five continents united by sport. The colours of blue, black, red, yellow and green were chosen because apparently there's not a flag in the world without at least one of these colours. It is a very neat symbol of the internationalism of sport at its best.

But throughout Olympic history the Five Rings have on occasion been identified with other things too, including male chauvinism, imperial power, German Nazism, Soviet Communism, the Cold War and big business. However, nowhere in this book will you find the suggestion that the Olympics are bad: it is what they have been turned into that I am against.

Hosting the Games will be for most a once-in-a-lifetime

experience. Few of us will still be around should the Olympics ever come to Great Britain again. The ambition should surely be to extend this experience to as many as possible and ensure that it is as memorable as it can be. Can anew Five Rings be imagined to fulfil the scale of this ambition? My argument in this chapter is that a better Olympics can be imagined, and that the version of the Olympics that London 2012 has produced falls very far short of reaching the scale of popular participation in the Games that was possible to achieve.

Each Games is shaped by the era in which it takes place. Our era has left its mark on the Olympics with the primacy of TV markets, the commercialization, the unreal and unchallenged rhetoric of legacy and participation, the disconnect with large segments of the host population and the ubiquitous security operation. But there is no force of nature or iron law of logic that requires the Olympics to assume their current shape. The Five Rings symbol has become associated with one particular model of global sport framed by these features, each of which is neither inevitable nor irreversible. The host city administrations, the governments and the sporting authorities have failed to offer any kind of alternative, any sort of challenge to corporate Olympism. That doesn't mean one can't be created, and in the process of imagining what a different sort of Olympics might look like we also begin to expose and challenge some of the dominant ideas of our period.

My 'New Five Rings' are based on five principles. First, decentralize the Games – no longer hold them in one city but across a region, a nation or even across different countries. Second, focus on maximizing participation, being part of the Olympics, as the core organizing principle. Third, relocate major parts of the event outside of the stadia, making them free-to-watch. Fourth, choose the sports contested based on their potential for universal accessibility. Fifth, disconnect the Olympics from corporate interests.

Is this hopelessly idealistic? Yes, in the same way that idealism inspired Baron de Coubertin to establish the modern Olympics in the first place. Despite all the flaws of its eventual implementation de Coubertin's vision was fundamentally idealistic. And yes, my proposal is politically motivated, because all sport is political. A better Games for all should have been the mission of London 2012. If the reality fails to measure up to this aim then something fundamental must be wrong with the entire concept, as conceived by both the current IOC and Seb Coe's London Organising Committee of the Olympic and Paralympic Games (LOCOG).

RING ONE: DECENTRALIZE THE OLYMPICS BY HOSTING THEM IN A NATION, NOT A CITY

When Baron de Coubertin founded the modern Olympic Movement his personal vision, written into the first Olympic

Charter of 1894 was for the Games to bring together the sporting youth of the world. The idea, which remains to this day, was that athletes would not just compete at the Games but would live together during the duration of the event. If young athletes from across the globe could get along for a fortnight or so it was hoped this would in some way lessen the likelihood of their nations going to war with each other. History had other plans, but this worthy ideal of a sporting peaceful coexistence was the basis for the 'Olympic Village'. This concept necessitates virtually all the Games' events to be situated in one city, with every venue easily reached from the athletic halls of residence. Thus Baron de Coubertin's sporting dream has been turned into concrete reality. More than any other factor, this concentration of the Games in one city ensures that as the Olympics grow in size the viability of the promises made on their behalf decline. Almost all the broken promises of the modern Games flow from this centralization and all the alternatives are facilitated by its opposite, decentralization.

Today none of the original purpose of the Olympic Village applies. Elite sport is now entirely different to what it looked like in the early twentieth century. Most athletes will stay in their own nation's squad camps until a day or so before competing. In 2008 Team GB stayed in Macau, and in 2004, Cyprus – nowhere near either Beijing or Athens. Most athletes fly in from afar to stay in the Olympic Village for just a day or so before competing, and once their particular competition is over the highly commodified competitors are often too busy fulfilling sponsor and broadcasting commitments to do much mixing in the cause of world peace.

The latest version of the Olympic Charter simply says that the Village meets the 'objective of bringing together all competitors, team officials and other team personnel in one place.' The warm, if frankly meaningless, words about world peace are long gone, but the dogma of centralization remains, which suits the interests of the IOC. Basing the entire Olympic programme in one city principally serves the IOC's vanity project. The well-staffed bureaucracy of the IOC stays in the finest city-centre hotels, with the global corporate business class of sponsors in their tow. Together they will be transported to one venue after another in their fleets of chauffeur-driven limousines. They will have no time to waste and will tolerate no inconvenience. Every Games is franchized out to a host city to be organized within the strictest possible parameters set by the IOC. Fulfilling the IOC's highly centralized vision of what the Games should look like is the first requirement of the local organizing committee.

Each Olympics is hosted in just one city, not an entire nation, despite the close and necessary involvement of national governments and other national bodies. Compare this to the football, rugby or cricket World Cups, in which games are played all

over a country and sometimes in more than one nation. These
versions of sporting mega-events can have their problems too.
On occasion stadia are built with no obvious post–World Cup
use and capacities increased to levels that will never be filled
again. But in the case of all of Great Britain, not just London,
hosting the Olympics this most certainly wouldn't have been
the case.

In England we already have enough of a problem with the
centralization of sport. London 2012 will simply make this
problem worse. European countries that are immeasurably
more successful at football than England in terms of their
World Cup and European championship records manage
to get by perfectly well without a national football stadium.
Germany, France, Italy, Spain and Holland use club grounds
for international matches. Where a national stadium does exist
it is not used for all international games. Wembley's contract
means that every England international will be played there for
the first three decades of the stadium's life, as well as FA Cup
semifinals and finals and the Championship, League One and
League Two playoffs. The purpose is not to suit the fans but to
reduce Wembley's huge operating loss. While Wembley was
closed from 2000 to 2007 during the hugely expensive rebuild-
ing, the biggest experiment in English football devolution was
forced upon the FA, and it proved to be highly successful. An
England football international finally became a local game, not

only for the immense conurbations of Greater Manchester, Merseyside, the North East and the West Midlands, but also for grounds in Ipswich, Southampton, Derby and Leicester.

In rugby all England internationals are played at Twickenham in London. Two cricket test matches in any series will always be played in London, at Lord's and the Oval. Britain's only tennis grand slam tournament takes place at Wimbledon, also in London. For any nation the Olympics only come around once in a generation, if that. So why on earth restrict it to just one city? The most basic way to address the broken Olympic promises of participation, regeneration and legacy is to replace the host Olympic city with a host Olympic nation.

Across Great Britain Glasgow, Edinburgh, Cardiff, Manchester, Liverpool, Newcastle, Birmingham, Leeds, Sheffield and Nottingham have the existing capacity in the shape of stadia, arenas and other facilities to host major parts of the Olympics. With an imaginative programme for the Games few new facilities would need to be built. Where investment in new venues could be justified by projected future use they may constitute a legitimate expense, but the main objective of an Olympic bid would be to make the best use of existing resources across the entire country.

Such devolution would have two distinctive impacts. First, the live audience in the stands would be characterized mainly by its locality. Olympic events could be used to creatively mobilize a city and region's population via a civic and regional pride in sport, actively linked to participation projects. Second, those parts of Britain which enjoy nothing like London's profile as a tourist destination would be afforded the kind of global platform that the Olympics is supposed to provide. Many of these cities won't be nearly as familiar as London to the world's media and the global audience.

With 26 Olympic sports to choose from cities and regions would be allocated those parts of the Games that would best suit existing facilities, established by an audit which would be a required part of the bidding process. Currently almost the entire emphasis is placed on building from scratch the most ambitious and extravagant new facilities, which over and over again prove to be grossly underused almost as soon as the Games are over. The problem of finding legacy-use for these facilities is exacerbated by their concentration in one place where they are not necessarily most needed.

Many of the sports featured at London 2012 scarcely have any media profile. Outside of the Olympic cycle virtually no backpage, TV or radio coverage is provided for trampolining, archery, badminton, hockey, judo, taekwondo and more. Through decentralization each participating city or region could become a host for a designated Olympic sport. An ambitious programme could be launched stretching from elite preparation to grassroots participation. Schools would be key.

Each school could adopt its city's Olympic sport and run a seven-year scheme between the successful bid and the Games. Team GB's squad for each sport would be based in the relevant city or region throughout the buildup, adding outreach coaching work to their activities to root their medal ambitions in the local communities. This would provide hands-on inspiration, linking beginners to the elite. Participation in the sport and ticket sales would be closely connected, with the Games starting to feel like something that belonged to all, not just to some. And instead of money being poured into one big-bang London opening ceremony, each host city or region could put on their own event for their sport and the athletes from all around the world taking part.

Such a process at least begins to place popular participation in the Games at the centre of the Olympic vision. The Olympics would be brought closer to the people. The model would be flexible to local circumstances – other Games might be hosted by regions, or even a mix of countries, such as a Benelux or Balkan Olympics. Abandoning the centralization that underpins London 2012 and all other recent Olympics would provide a much bigger opportunity for people to be part of the Games, to share in its benefits and spread its costs. A decentralized model for the Games is the first essential New Ring to help us imagine the better Olympics that London 2012 might have been.

RING TWO: USE VENUES THAT MAXIMIZE THE
NUMBER OF TICKETS AVAILABLE

Unless live participation is adopted as the core organizing principle of a 'home' Games it loses most of the special impact it might have had on the host nation's population, and the Olympics might as well be taking place anywhere in the world. The fact that TV coverage will be even more blanket than usual and giant screens will be erected all over the place is a poor substitute for the opportunity to be there, in the stadium, the velodrome or beside the pool, watching the action.

The Olympic Games consist in the main of sports with little or no international travelling fanbase. Instead most of the demand for tickets to the Games is domestic. The number of live spectators should be maximized to turn the Games into a genuinely national event of which as many people as possible can be a part. A happy consequence might be to help fulfil the Olympic promise of increasing participation in sport. Actually being at the Olympics has surely more of a chance of inspiring us to get active, compared to watching it all from the comfort of our own sofas.

The row over the availability of London 2012 tickets was entirely predictable. From the euphoria of the successful bid in July 2005 right up to the opening of the complex ticket-application procedure, the public was more or less told that all they had to do was register, apply and pay up and the tickets would be in the post. With an advertising, PR and media campaign that dwarfed any previous sporting or entertainment event in British history, demand was always guaranteed to out-strip supply. In addition a huge percentage of the prime event tickets were allocated to the IOC and corporate sponsors. The media entourage take another gigantic chunk out of a stadium's capacity, which is reduced still further by all the many extra TV camera positions and big screens. Such has been the fate of all major sporting events for at least the past three decades, and London 2012 did nothing to change this. The dominant priority in organizing the Games is the production of a TV spectacular, with the spectators providing little more than background colour. Ticket income is important, but given the choice the organizers prefer to sell fewer tickets at a higher price than more at a lower price.

Of course the global TV audience will be far bigger than the live crowd. But are the interests of those watching worldwide in their living rooms and those in the stadium of necessity mutu-ally exclusive? As for sponsors' enormous ticket allocations, the IOC and the LOCOG have sold the Olympics short. A reduction of the number of reserved tickets from thousands to a handful would be unlikely to cause sponsors to pull out, most need the Games too much to do so, and those that did leave could swiftly be replaced.

Massively reducing the sponsors' and media entourage's

ticket allocations would go some way to increasing the numbers who could actually watch the Games live. But the key is to link the first of our New Rings, decentralization, to our second new ring, participation. Ticket availability could have been vastly increased by taking stock of all of the country's largest stadia, indoor arenas and outdoor spaces and adapting them where necessary. For example, instead of holding show jumping at Greenwich Park with a capacity of 23,000, the Millennium Stadium in Cardiff could be used with a capacity more than three times that number, 72,500. For hockey a new stadium has been built within the Olympic Park, capacity 15,000. Instead hockey, which is played as a kind of mini World Cup with 12 teams in each of the men's and women's tournaments, could be played across a region in a variety of much larger stadia. For example Yorkshire and Humberside boasts stadia in Huddersfield, Leeds, Sheffield, Bradford and Doncaster all considerably larger than 15,000. An Olympic hockey tourna-ment organized in this way would also permit a larger number of nations to compete. For boxing the ExCelcentre, which holds 32,000 people, will host the Olympic competition. Ricky Hatton's defence of his International Boxing Organization World Light Welterweight title against Juan Lazcano was fought at Manchester City's stadium, capacity 45,000. The blue half of the city might not like it but there's no reason why Manchester United's Old Trafford, capacity 75,000, couldn't host the boxing semi-finals and finals with a combination of Manchester City's stadium and the MEN Arena, capacity 21,000, coping with the less popular earlier rounds.

A look down the list of some of the other Olympic sports – basketball, handball, fencing, judo, taekwondo, weightlifting, wrestling, dressage, beach volleyball – reveals many that could be successfully held in existing, mainly football, stadia, with far higher crowd capacity than the facilities being built for 2012. More radical thinking might be required for the swimming events, which include water polo and synchronized swimming. The current Aquatic Centre will have a capacity of 17,500 for diving and swimming, reduced to 5,000 for water polo. An alternative option might have been to locate the swimming events in a region, say the West Midlands, and build a network of open-air pools at significantly reduced cost with temporary stands. At previous Games pools have often been in the open-air. With Birmingham, Wolverhampton and Coventry sharing the various swimming disciplines the crowds able to attend could have been vastly increased. A three- or four-fold multiplication of the legacy facilities could have been produced at a fraction of the cost of the Stratford pool. It is also somewhat bizarre that the hugely popular swimming events only utilize the Olympic pool for the first week of the Games. This is a product of the pre-digital TV age when too many finals competing for attention would have defeated a channel's ability to broadcast them. Now we have many more channels and the 'red button'. Using the multi-pool model I am suggesting swimming could have been extended and expanded over the entire two weeks, increasing both numbers who could have attended and the number of athletes taking part. An example of imaginative thinking from London's 1948 Olympics is worth taking note of too. Wembley's Empire Pool was used for these Games. It was subsequently drained of water and turned into a hugely successful and profitable live venue, mainly for music – an ingenious way of making another use of a facility that otherwise might have been under-used, left derelict or demolished.

As for the Olympic Stadium, before this was built London already had three stadia with a capacity over 60,000: Twickenham, Wembley and Arsenal's Emirates Stadium. All three of these super-size stadia could have been reconfigured to hold various parts of the track-and-field programme, requiring considerably less investment than building a new stadium in Stratford. Indeed, most of the front half of the pitch-level seats at Wembley can be removed: they are retracted to accommodate a stage for a music concert. On other occasions the Wembley pitch has been covered to suit motor racing. So why not make use of Wembley, with its capacity of 92,000, for Olympic events other than football? Twickenham and the Emirates likewise have proven flexibility: they have both hosted rock concerts. Yet neither one of them is being used at all for the Olympics despite Twickenham having a capacity of 82,000 and the Emirates, 60,000. Again, bizarre pre-digital programming means the Olympic Stadium is scarcely used for the first week of the Games, except for the opening ceremony. Sharing athletics across three stadia would have given the same two-fold benefit as for the swimming: more people in the stands, and more athletes from a greater spread of countries.

Of course a football or rugby stadium isn't immediately ideal for many of the sports I'm suggesting could be held there. Covering would need to be laid over the grass to create a surface on which to lay AstroTurf for the hockey; a sprung wooden floor for the basketball, volleyball and handball; sand for the beach volleyball; raised stages with suitable surfaces for boxing, fencing, judo and taekwondo and weightlifting. Pitches would have to be relaid for the new season after these different sports had done their damage. Seating would need to be arranged closer to the action for events that do not use the whole field. Some events would be at the mercy of the elements, requiring the kind of flexibility seen at Wimbledon in June when it rains (although heavy rain for days on end is considerably less likely during late July and early August). None of these problems is insurmountable. Nor would they cost anything like as much to solve as the act of building all new stadia, of doubtful post-Olympic viability yet with unambitious capacities that serve to keep out many who might otherwise have attended the Olympics for the first and only times in their lives. What a waste of money and opportunity.

The one London 2012 sport that will be using existing stadia around the country is football. And it has proved the most difficult to sell tickets for. I would argue this is for three reasons. First, interest in the Olympic football tournament has been next to nil in Great Britain historically. No Team GB football team has been entered in the Games since 1972, when it was an amateur team. Each of the home nations – England, Scotland and Wales – proudly competes in football individually; and in football no Team GB concept existed until it was reinvented for the sake of the 2012 football tournament. Second, and as a result, the Olympic tournament isn't even seen in Britain as a downmarket alternative to the World Cup and European Championships, but as a distant and irrelevant event in the football calendar. And third, the football tournament, and for different reasons the Olympic yachting based in Weymouth, are the exceptions to the centralization of London 2012. There is no narrative to connect it to a broader strategy projecting the Games as a national event. Instead the odd football match in Glasgow, Cardiff, Manchester and elsewhere is widely viewed in Scotland, Wales and the English regions as not much more than a token gesture.

Rather than a one-off, my idea is to connect the first two

Rings – decentralization and participation – to create a national celebration of sport with umpteen local components. The venues' much bigger crowd capacities should translate into significantly reduced ticket prices. For the crucial audience of children, schemes would allow schools to send kids to the Games for free. It is the 2012 generation, the first-timers to the Olympics in their country, for whom this might be a life-changing experience. A Games centred on their mass participation, in city after city, would be a truly worthwhile collective venture.

The Olympics in marketing terms is one of the world's great brands. The Five Rings are universally recognizable and associated with some of the most iconic moments in world sport. This is what would make such an ambitious plan possible to fulfil; no other sporting event short of football's World Cup has anything like the same potential to draw in and be shared by such a large percentage of the population.

RING THREE: RELOCATE SPORTS OUTSIDE THE STADIA TO CREATE FREE-TO-WATCH EVENTS

A decentralized Olympics with the aim of the widest possible participation from spectators is a good start. My third New Ring is a commitment to remove as many sports as possible from the stadia, making them free to watch.

Some of the most joyful sporting events don't take place

within specially designed buildings at all. The London Marathon, the Great North Run and other road races around the world, the Tour de France, the Oxford and Cambridge Boat Race on the River Thames – all are free to watch, with no ticket required. These events engage with an existing environment and in most cases involve a popular participation element. A Games which relocated large parts of the programme from private to public spaces would be more accessible and festive than any Olympic Stadium spectacle can be.

One of the most shameful decisions Seb Coe made in the implementation of the Games programme was to change the planned route of the marathon, one of the few existing Olympic competitions that takes place outside a stadium. In London's original bid the marathon was to be run around the East End – it was claimed that such wonderful exposure would directly aid the economic regeneration of this neglected part of the city. This marathon route would certainly have represented a rare opportunity for Tower Hamlets, Newham, Hackney and Waltham Forest to provide the background scenery to the Games. For much of the rest of the time the TV cameras will be focused on the action in the pool, on the track, round the velodrome. With the Olympic Park isolated from its surrounding environment the East End will be largely invisible to TV viewers. But the marathon was the exception, and with a sizeable chunk of the annual London Marathon route already passing through the East End the area had some experience of hosting a high-profile road race.

But in 2010 all of that changed. Coe announced that the entire race would be run in a loop taking in Buckingham Palace, St Paul's, Admiralty Arch and the Houses of Parliament – landmarks most of the world is already familiar with. This decision is emblematic of the IOC and LOCOG's lack of interest in expanding the reach of the Games in the way my third New Ring would do. The new four-lap route reduces the number that can spectate from the pavement without a ticket by three-quarters. An A-to-B route such as the London Marathon provides 26.2 miles of pavement on both sides of the road, plus bridges, pubs and numerous other vantage points. The Olympic marathon loop has barely 6 miles of pavement to watch from for free. The same criticisms can be levelled at the triathlon, for which both the running and cycling elements will consist of multiple laps of a loop.

A loop layout also precludes any mass participation element. The elite racers would be continuously tripping over the club and fun runners as they lapped them over and over again, as opposed to the London Marathon style A-to-B route where the racers leave the rest miles behind and neither gets in the way of the other. The London Marathon every year proves that it is entirely manageable to combine one of the most elite competitions in sport, often run in world record–breaking time, with a race open to tens of thousands of club runners and recreational joggers. London 2012 is so lacking in any ambition that such a project was only briefly considered and then promptly jettisoned for no apparent reason. The potential for disruptive protests is obviously one concern, but if the organizers surrender every opportunity to open up the Olympics because of security fears, then the whole point of hosting the Games at all is fatally undermined.

Although the Olympic 20km and 50km walks do not have quite the same appeal as the marathon, they are also races that can be watched for free from the pavement. However, once again London 2012 chose a central London loop, up and down the Mall, breaking the connection with the East End still further and massively reducing the number that will see the race, for free.

Maximizing the numbers that can watch for free should be the beginning of a transformation of the Olympic programme. When the marathon was adopted as part of the inaugural Games in 1896, long-distance road running was a minority, eccentric pursuit. But since the early 1980s road running has become hugely popular. By adding an Olympic half-marathon the Games would both reflect this popularity and provide another free event to watch. A 10km road race could also replace one of the least attractive of the track races for spectators, the 25 laps of the circuit that make up the 10,000m.

At least the Olympic road cycling events aren't using this lap format. Races will be cycled over a single circuit for their total distance and as a result have the potential to attract the largest possible number to watch mostly for free. The routes will pass through a whole range of communities, although they will once more studiously avoid London's East End and its suburban hinterland, instead heading out towards the leafy villages, lanes and hills of Surrey. But cycling will only feature as a single day's racing and a time trial. A multistage race spanning the duration of the Olympics, modelled on the Tour de France, could bring the furthest decentralization possible, reaching not only every corner of the host nation but also stretching into neighbouring countries. The numbers able to watch for free would be staggeringly high, and the daily stages would form a powerful sporting narrative throughout the Games with a climactic final stage to close the event.

Once every four years the Team GB rowers win a hatful of Gold medals, but the only other time the British public takes any interest in the sport is the annual Oxford and Cambridge Boat Race on the River Thames. This spectacle is watched for free by an estimated 250,000 spectators lining the riverbank and bridges. The Olympic rowing facility at Eton Dorney has a capacity just 30,000. The Thames would be unsuitable for the events in the current Olympic rowing programme, but why not add another based on the Boat Race? Tidal patterns and the width of the river would narrow any competition programme to two crews racing at a time and not much more than four races per day. A knockout competition staged over the entire Olympic period could provide daily races to watch, attracting huge numbers with no ticket required, with a climactic finish on a final day when the two finalists would battle it out for Gold.

Another event that might be considered is a canoe marathon, raced on a river over the distance of 40 kilometres, or a multistage race like the annual Devizes to Westminster International Canoe Race, which attracts hundreds of crews each year. Again it would be free to watch with a potentially enormous audience lining the riverbank, in the latter case stretching over 125 miles.

All the yachting events at the 2012 Olympics will be based in Weymouth. But every four years a race around Britain of two-handed boats is held in cities, lasting some seven days. Imagine an Olympic event that visited Lowestoft, Barra on the Western Isles and Lerwick on Shetland, with Plymouth for the start and finish. The quaysides of ports and harbours would be heaving with spectators, the sea full of welcoming flotillas of small boats as each day's racing comes to an end.

The centralization of the Olympics has a further consequence for those events that usually depend on the use of the natural environment. With the exception of yachting, because so many Olympics are held nowhere near the sea, inferior locations within easy reach of the host city must be used even if far superior courses are available elsewhere in the country. This is true of equestrian three-day eventing, the canoe slalom, outdoor swimming and mountain biking among others. These events are customarily watched from the course, but by using custom-built facilities for the Olympics crowds will be reduced considerably.

For example Badminton is one of the most famous three-day eventing courses in the world, with a spectator capacity that significantly exceeds the facility built especially for London 2012 at Greenwich Park. This will mean an event in which Team GB has traditionally done very well will be watched by fewer people than would have been the case if the existing facility had been used, just because all events need to take place in the one city.

London has no natural whitewater river course suitable for the canoe slalom, so at an estimated cost of £30 million an artificial facility was built at Waltham Cross in the Lee Valley. Natural courses do abound across Britain, and some in North Wales have hosted world and European competitions. These venues have drawbacks – they would be out of the way and in this instance would possibly have lower crowd capacity – but the compensation would be the financial savings from not having to construct a purpose-built installation. Such events would also be far more accessible to the local population, with the additional advantage of providing a profile for natural features which could help attract tourists, who might not have been aware of these places, long after the Olympics are over.

Open water swimming is a relatively new Olympic discipline, featured for the first time as part of the triathlon in 2000, and in its own right at Beijing eight years later. The 10-kilometre race will be swum in London's Hyde Park Serpentine, which is hardly 'open water' in the true sense, whereas the Lake District or any of Scotland's lochs could have provided a wonderful scenic location with plenty of space to watch for free on and off the water.

Mountain biking is another sport for which London is not naturally suited. There aren't any mountains in or around London, so a modest course has been built in Essex, a county that in the main isn't even very hilly. The Scottish Highlands, Pennines or North Wales could all have provided far more challenging, natural race venues and once more gained an international profile in the process.

There is a broader point about using the natural environment. Olympic sports are not fixed – they come and go as a result of IOC votes – so there is no reason why the natural assets of the host nation should not shape the Games programme. With some excellent off road cycling routes a mountain biking trail race could have been added to the existing descent event for the British Games. The Lake District could have held a trail running event, combining cross-country with aspects of fell running and the mountain marathon. Newquay could have hosted surfing, a sport with which it is now associated the world over. Mountain biking, trail running and surfing are considerably more popular sports than some other Olympic disciplines, capable of pulling in a crowd and with no need for stadia. But they are excluded thanks to the IOC's unchallenged model of what an Olympic Games should look like.

Roads and open country, mountains, rivers, beaches and the sea; these are the natural features Britain possesses which could provide the settings for large parts of a refashioned Olympic programme. It would mean some changes to what is on offer, I would argue for the better. But it would make a powerful statement about sport as a legitimate and welcome occupant of public space, truly rooting the Olympics in places and communities. Of course achieving this depends entirely on our first New Ring – decentralization – even if all these public events could somehow be held in London the entire city would have to be shut down for the duration of the Games.

This plan would have another significant advantage. When the London Marathon is run it incorporates not just club and fun runners alongside the elite athletes but also a whole series of child and youth mini-marathon races run on the same course as the main event. On the Tour de France one stage each year is chosen as the Etape du Tour – a day when the professionals' route is open to the general public, attracting over 8,500 participants. Using these two brilliantly imaginative innovations as a model to extend to other events, the Olympics could be opened up for us not just to watch but to take part in too. One of the most attractive examples could be to invite spectators of the 20- and 50-kilometre walk events to stroll 10 kilometres down the roads closed to traffic after the athletes have passed and claim a medal of their own – a delightfully simple way to start the fulfilment of the Olympic participation promise.

If all this sounds rather quaint and antiquated consider this: our consumption of sport has been transformed by a permanent communications revolution. A national press, the telegraph and the telephone first made possible newspaper coverage of international sport. Next, radio and cinema newsreels, followed by TV in black and white and eventually colour, then multiple satellite channels and finally digital TV brought sport into the home. The internet provided a new media platform, while the mobile phone complete with camera turned us all into full-time photographers. Now, that phone has become a mobile television too. Once, standing by the roadside watching a runner or cyclist pass by meant seeing the merest fragment of a race. Now, we can mix the thrill of being a part of the Olympics on the pavement, the riverbank or the mountainside with a TV in our pocket to ensure we get a full picture of the day's competition. Moving sport out of the stadia isn't a romantic step backwards; it's a very modern step forward that keeps pace with technological change.

RING FOUR: CHOOSE SPORTS ON THE BASIS OF THEIR UNIVERSAL ACCESSIBILITY

The list of Olympic sports for London 2012 numbers 26. The selection has changed considerably over the history of the Games. Athletics, swimming, fencing and various versions of gymnastics have been the only ever-presents. Powerboat racing, croquet and the Basque game pelota are among those that have made only one-off appearances.

To suggest that the Olympic medals table should be weighted by GDP or population size would be for me a step too far in changing what international competitive sport purports to stand for. But at the same time if no consideration is given to the lack of universal access to the sports accorded Olympic status then any Medals Table is distorted out of all meaning.

The IOC already acknowledges this to a degree. Selected sports have to prove they are widely practised around the world – an entirely justifiable condition. Yet if in some sports the medals are only ever won by a tiny handful of mainly rich nations, while entire continents have never come close to winning, then just how useful is that criteria?

Of all the medals awarded in rowing since Los Angeles 1984 just one has been won by an African nation – South Africa's lone Bronze at Athens 2004. None at all have gone to South America or any country from Asia. Sailing is a similar picture. Since 1984 not a single African nation has won a sailing medal, while only Brazil and Argentina from South America, and Japan and China from Asia have sailing medals to their names. As for the equestrian events, since 1984 there have been no African medallists, and just one Bronze for Saudi Arabia from Asia, with only Brazil flying the flag for South America.

For many other Olympic sports the picture is more or less the same. In fencing there has not been one medallist from either Africa or South America since 1984, and just one each for South Korea and Japan from all of Asia. In cycling no medals have gone to Africa or South America, while only Japan and China have won for all of Asia. Canoeing has rewarded Africa with a solitary medal, for Togo, since 1984, and one for Asia in the form of China, while South America has got none.

In contrast the men's football Gold medallists between 1984 and 2008 have been split between Argentina (twice), France, the former USSR, Spain, Nigeria and Cameroon. Of the Silver medals Brazil has won two, with the rest going to Yugoslavia, Spain, Poland, Nigeria, Argentina and Paraguay. Germany, Ghana, Chile and Italy have picked up a Bronze medal each. Football is the most universal of all the Olympic team sports. A ball can be made out of anything, a match played on almost any surface, by teams of almost any size. Goals can be painted on a wall, made from a pair of oil drums, or in the classic instance of childhood football, jumpers for goalposts. The rules are uncomplicated, with the obvious exception of the offside rule, which few people, including most referees, fully understand. Any footwear can be worn, or none. No particular physical attributes are required – world-class footballers come in all shapes and sizes. And since football has been globalized the migration of players from poor countries to rich ones can be exploitative but for the lucky few it is also the route to great riches. This has been accompanied by the global communications revolution, with national leagues watched on TV screens the world over.

It is puzzling, then, that the Olympic football tournament enjoys such a low profile. This observation is partly Anglocentric, but it is undeniable that football's own global tournament, the World Cup, is so much bigger and more important to players, coaches and fans than the Olympic version.

The Olympic football tournament could be so much better. One way to improve it would be to tap into the FIFA age-group World Cups, which currently enjoy little or no profile. With FIFA's cooperation men's and women's Olympic football could be combined with an Under-21 World Cup. Already the Olympic tournament enforces player age restrictions so why not make this more of a virtue? And why limit the tournament to just 16 nations when this is the one team sport that almost every Olympic nation plays? In contrast to other sports like handball, volleyball (both varieties), basketball and hockey, the medal-winners in football are as likely to come from Africa, South America and Asia as from Europe and North America. If it was organised as a 48-team competition this would make the Olympic Under-21 World Cup the largest international football tournament of all. To facilitate so many matches the competition would have to be extended over an entire month, but the 2012 tournament already starts a few days before the opening ceremony so why not? Such a change in the way the Olympic football tournament is organized, for the women too, would preserve the primacy of the World Cup for FIFA and provide an Olympic competition with a distinctive and attractive character of its own.

In terms of the spread of nations winning medals, boxing is among the most accessible of Olympic sports. Since 1984 there have been a total of 69 Gold medals to be won. The victors have come from 20 different countries, from every continent. The USA tops the Gold medal table with 14, followed by Cuba with 13, Russia with 9, Kazakhstan with 5 and South Korea and Thailand with 4 each. Africa is represented by Golds for Kenya and Algeria. Australasia and Oceania have had success through Silvers for Australia, New Zealand and Tonga. The total number of nations to win a boxing medal from 1984 to 2008 is a staggering 57. Hardly any other Olympic sport comes anywhere close to this. This is a global sport with a powerful and rich professional version, yet Olympic boxing retains a very high status.

The major powers in boxing have changed over time. The sport has seen the rise of Central American, Southeast Asian, Cuban, African and Black Sea nations at various times, but few have ended up dominating one weight division, and certainly none the whole tournament. In middle and long-distance running, from 1948 to 1964 there were a total of 30 Gold medals to be won by male athletes. In distances from 800m upwards, three were won by the USA, three by New Zealand, one by Australia, one by Argentina, and the rest by European nations. This was apart from Africa's two solitary medals, won by Ethiopia's Abebe Bikila, victor in the 1960 and 1964 Olympic Marathons. Aside from these Golds, up to 1968 only two other African athletes had won any medals in these distance events. But Bikila's success was a sign of races to come.

From 1984 to 2008 African nations won three out of the seven men's 800m Golds; five out of seven at 1,500m; six out of seven at 5,000m; six out of seven at 10,000m; and Kenya alone has won every 3,000m steeplechase race in this period. Out of seven marathon Golds three were also claimed by African nations.

In the women's events African dominance has been less, but still impressive: two out of the seven 800m Golds; three out of seven at 1,500m; two out of four at 5,000m; three out of six at 10,000m; and one out of seven in the marathon.

At Beijing in 2008 the continent's growing dominance could not have been more apparent. In the men's 800m, 5,000m, 10,000m and marathon African nations scored a clean sweep of all the medals. In the 3,000m steeplechase they picked up Gold and Bronze, and in the 1,500m they got Gold. The rise of African women at these distances was becoming much more obvious too. They achieved a clean sweep in the 800ms, Gold and Bronze in the 5,000m, Gold in the 1,500m and 10,000m, and Silver in the 3,000m steeplechase and the marathon.

Football, boxing, middle- and long-distance running each offer a window on a future for the Games that is rooted in the universal accessibility of sport. Organized club athletics and road and cross-country running retain a significant grassroots and elite presence in most European countries and the United States. Yet some of the poorest countries in the world including Ethiopia, Kenya, Burundi, Morocco, Algeria and Mozambique have all won Olympic Golds in the middle and long distances, while Eritrean athlete Zersenay Tadese also holds the world records at the non-Olympic distances of 25kms and the half-marathon. What distance running has in common with football and boxing is that it is a simple sport. No special kit is required – it is entirely possible to run barefoot and be at no significant disadvantage provided the soles of your feet have been sufficiently hardened. It is not necessary to be of a particular physical build as endurance and speed are mostly the result of ever-increasing mileages, sprint training and freedom from injury. As writer Adharanand Finn has detailed in his superb book *Running with the Kenyans*, a tradition of running decent distances to school and back from an early age, the soft surface of the trails, which reduces the risk of impact injuries through wear and tear, and a high-carb low-fat diet are key. Other elements may also be at play, such as the altitude in some parts of Africa, mountainous terrain and, more controversially, genetics, but they are not definitive in determining success as an elite runner.

None of these factors behind Black African athletes' success are the result of a high GDP; in fact the opposite is more likely to be the case. But it is the cash nexus of world professional athletics that has transformed such advantages into the basis on which to produce world-beating male and female distance runners. While Africa's first successes pre-date professionalization, the financial bonanza now available for those who can run fastest provides the impetus to African athletes to compete and dominate their sport. Finn describes it neatly: 'Poverty exists in many other places, and the will to escape is not unique to Kenyans. The difference, however, is that in Kenya, that will is channelled into running. Every last drop of it.' This is not to romanticize poverty, far from it, but the enormous success of Kenyan, Ethiopian and other African nations' athletes does suggest that running is a great sporting leveller.

An equalizing process in the Olympic programme would seek to increase those events that require fewer resources. Distance running is at the core of this ambition, so apart from adding the half-marathon and trail running, a road relay and further endurance events could be introduced. The human body is not limited to the marathon; in fact recreational runners now complete marathons with relative ease. Why not add the classic further distance of the 100kms, and a 24-hour team relay with the aim of recording the highest number of laps of of a circuit within that time?

But the bigger solution is for the IOC to introduce new sports to the Olympics with the express purpose of equalizing access to participation and competition. Too many medals in Olympic sports are won over and over again by the same countries. In most cases this is down to the expense of the facilities and the preparation required to get their athletes into a winning position, as well as the narrow social class that plays those sports. In some cases it is also due to the need for regular access to particular natural features to practice. Some sports require specific physical features to excel. Becoming an Olympic sport is not only a source of prestige: it also opens up the opportunity of commercial sponsorship and government funding. Those sports that fail to broaden their universal access should be warned that they might lose their treasured Olympic status. And in their place the IOC should seek out new sports that do have the capacity to be universal.

How about a former Olympic sport that has not been contested at a Games since 1920: the tug-of-war? It is hard to think of a team sport that requires fewer resources – just a sturdy rope. The event could feature mixed male and female teams and would be far more watchable than some current Olympic sports.

One sport that would meet the criteria is darts. Unfairly maligned by a snobbish sports establishment and media as non-exercise for fat blokes who drink and smoke as they compete, darts in fact can be compared with Olympic target sports like shooting and archery. But unlike these sports no expensive kit or special facilities are required, just a dartboard and set of darts.

Another sport which could be given a trial for Olympic recognition might be Orienteering. In all three cases, Tug-of-War, Darts and Orienteering there is little or no need for expensive kit or facilities, no access to very particular natural features is required, special body types don't provide an unnatural advantage, the rules are relatively simple and the social appeal is potentially broad. And if these new Olympic sports fail to prove over one or two Olympic cycles that they can reach a level of popularity and improving standards of performance in a wide variety of countries they should be dropped and other sports given a go on the same basis.

Promoting access to sport shouldn't necessarily be limited either to the track, the pool, the velodrome and other locations where the athletic contests will take place. In the early twentieth century an Olympic Games would also include medals for architecture, music, literature, sculpture and painting. The modern descendent of this is the Cultural Olympiad, which this year has been rebranded the London 2012 Festival due to the fear that no one would know what something cultural called an Olympiad could possibly be. Headline shows include Leona Lewis, Damien Hirst and a Shakespeare festival. Quite what X-Factor generated pop, dead sharks immersed in formaldehyde and early-modern theatre have to do with sport is not explained. The Olympics could have been the opportunity for a Cannes-style festival to choose the best film inspired by sport from an international entry list, a Turner style Prize for the best art with a sport theme, Booker type prizes for the best sports book, theatre and poetry. Olympic medals could be awarded for these too. If sport is to become truly accessible then culture has a vital part to play in its popularization. A Cultural Olympiad of this sort would be both truly special to the Olympics and could help to fulfil that all-important promise of inspiring participation in sport.

Sports that allow the widest possible access aren't downgraded competitions. There will still be a Gold medal to hang round the winner's neck, but the contest will be more equal and meaningful. An Olympic programme founded on the basis of the universal accessibility of sport will result in higher levels of athletic achievement. Competition and participation are complementary.

RING FIVE: A SYMBOL OF THE OLYMPICS NOT A LOGO FOR THE SPONSORS

The Olympic Five Rings is the only symbol used in international sports that is instantly recognizable the world over. Few would be able to sketch FIFA's insignia, know what the IAAF's looks like or even be aware if world boxing has a symbol to unify its various warring factions. Golf, rugby and cricket have a bewildering array of logos for various international contests, none of them very memorable. The US sports of American football, baseball and basketball have a global reach but are identified mainly by club badges, few with the international recognition of the five rings.

This ready recognizability is a product of tradition, longevity and the rarity-value of a quadrennial event. The Olympic Games have criss-crossed the globe to be held in Europe, North and Central America, Asia, Australasia and, coming in 2016, South America. The one glaring omission is Africa. Design has played a part – the best logos are delightfully simple, instantly memorable and easy to reproduce. The five rings is up there with McDonald's Golden arches, the Nike swoosh

and that distinctive curly writing Coca-Cola uses, as part of
the international marketing language of signs.

Sport has been transformed by globalization. Michael Jordan
was described by the writer Walter LaFeber as symbolizing the
rise of the new global capitalism in the 1990s. Golf's European
tour now stretches to Abu Dhabi. Formula 1 Grand Prix are
staged in China and India. The 2010 football World Cup was
held in Africa. Rugby union and cricket both boast World Cup
formats that just two decades ago didn't exist. The Premiership
is easily the most globalized institution in British society – the
clubs' owners, managers, coaches, players and fans come from
every continent on earth. The way the Olympics have changed
is very much part of this development, the impetus of which is
primarily economic.

Interconnected with globalization are changes in the media.
Across the world TV viewing habits have been revolutionized.
The multiplication of channels and the rise of the internet as
a main source of entertainment in the home have provided
choice but also massively fragmented the TV audience. Live
sport is one of the few exceptions to this trend, with a unique
capacity to reach a mass, global and youthful audience. Who
wants to watch the recorded highlights of the Olympic 100
metres, the Superbowl, or the Champions League final? These
events must be watched live, and as a result they retain the sense
of shared experience that elsewhere has been lost in a sea of

choice. Consequently sport has become central to maintaining and boosting broadcasters' audience and market share. Nothing else comes close. While football's World Cup achieves slightly higher TV viewing figures, in terms of worldwide audience appeal the grandest sports event of all remains the Olympics.

The process of commercialization has accelerated ever since the Los Angeles Games of 1984. The rising importance and influence accorded to corporate sponsors reflects ideological shifts in the wider world: the international neo-liberal consensus and the successful attempt to instil free market mantras as a form of unquestioned common sense. The list of Olympic 'Worldwide Partners' includes Coca-Cola, McDonald's, Samsung and Visa. London 2012's own official 'partners' feature Adidas, Lloyds TSB, BT and other mainly British companies. London 2012 Olympic 'supporters' include Cadbury and Thomas Cook, while the Olympic 'providers and suppliers' list Heineken, Holiday Inn and John Lewis among others. The vocabulary is interesting. Despite the triumph of the free market as a common sense for the 1990s and first half of the 2000s, most would recognise that these companies sponsor the Games purely for that these companies are in it for anything but commercial reasons. For them the Olympics is just another means of exposure and branding to shift products. Properly regulated there is nothing necessarily wrong with this, commercial interests have always aided the funding of the Games.

Dating back to those early twentieth century Olympics which were organised to coincide with international trade fairs. It's therefore important for get the language right. These aren't 'partners' or 'providers', they are companies acting as commercial sponsors, using the Games to their own ends.

As commercial interests have become more and more obvious the Games and the athletes are increasingly turned into billboards for the sponsors. But if we don't mind the Adidas logo looming so large on the Team GB kit that it appears as though Ennis, Hoy and Adlington are competing for a German manufacturer rather than good old Blighty, then we can probably live with this. Or if on arrival at the Olympic Park we find the food and drink on offer is strictly limited to McDonald's and Coca-Cola then for one day we may grudgingly sacrifice our freedom of choice. Finding that London 2012 tickets can only be bought with a Visa credit or debit card may be a bit of an imposition, but for most it is just another inconvenience thrown up by the way London 2012 has been organized, rather than an indictment of the rampaging greed of corporate power.

Such issues are largely a matter of taste, treated as a pain in the backside by many but tolerated nevertheless. But these individual grievances add up to a pattern. The sponsorship deals signed by the IOC and LOCOG have put the Olympics in the position of having to protect the commercial interests of the sponsors, regardless of the cost to the Olympic ethos. Within a week of London being awarded the Games, Parliament had introduced the London Olympics Bill, a new law which effectively privatized bits of the English language. 'Olympic', 'Olympics', 'Olympians' and 'Olympiad' became protected words, their use licensed by the London Games organizers. More words including 'Games', '2012' and 'Two Thousand and Twelve', if used in combination with 'London', 'Summer', 'Gold', 'Silver' and 'Bronze', were outlawed unless used by an approved sponsor. Clause 20 of the new law outlined the severe measures that potential language thieves would face:

A constable or enforcement officer may –

(a) enter land or premises on which they reasonably believe a contravention of regulations … is occurring;

(b) remove, destroy, conceal or erase any infringing article;

(c) when entering land under paragraph (a), be accompanied by one or more persons for the purpose of taking action under paragraph (b);

(d) use, or authorise the use of, reasonable force for the purpose of taking action under this subsection.

It would be wrong to be naïve; the major offenders in what

has become known as 'ambush marketing' are not small businesses or individuals but multinational companies who haven't signed the deals with the IOC and LOCOG and are looking to advertise and flog their goods unofficially. And in reality London will not be turned into some kind of dystopian nightmare city where the police search every nook and cranny for illicit words. But the new law does read like a newspeak protocol penned by George Orwell. The powerful forces that can legitimize legislation of this sort as an act of Olympian necessity are precisely those that insist on pretending the corporations that bankroll the Olympics are generous philanthropists, never in it just for the money, the truest friends of sport, who fully deserve the grateful thanks they have paid so much to receive.

The rise of the commercialization of sport is almost always presented as irresistible. In fact it is entirely resistible. In spite of the Olympics going professional most London 2012 competitors will be there because their excellence in sport provides them with pleasure, not heaps of money. The same is true of the many millions who participate in the same sports they see at the Olympics but who can only dream of reaching the standard necessary to compete at the Games. Sport remains a source of emotional, not financial, reward for the overwhelming proportion of those who do it. Away from the IOC, LOCOG and the top end of the major sports' governing bodies, the organizational culture of sport remains voluntary and free of self-interest.

This is a good starting point for the reorganization of the Olympics in a way that is driven by values rooted in popular participation and equal access, not commerce. In fact, if handled sensitively and imaginatively these values should not be the antithesis of commerce; rather they represent sport's version of the social market – a market that is both entrepreneurial yet socially useful, beneficial to all not just to some. My preceding four New Rings would result in key changes to the existing Games, each with the potential for the widest-possible economic benefit. First, using existing facilities wherever feasible and maximizing the use of the natural environment would slash new building costs and reduce the considerable risk of expensive maintenance bills for underused venues after the Games or, worse, the sale of failed stadia at a loss. Second, vastly increasing live audiences by combining the biggest available stadia and arenas with the lowest possible ticket prices could give a net gain in income. Third, by relocating a significant part of an extended Olympic programme outside the stadia an even bigger audience would be reached, with those who had been brought into the Games in this way being more likely to buy the official programme and T-shirt, as well as refreshments. This spending boost wouldn't just benefit the few companies licensed to trade in the Olympic Park, but would be spread far and wide to cities, towns and communities all over Britain. Fourth, by reconfiguring the selected sports to enhance their universal access and to create a more genuinely competitive world games, the global audience would have more of an emotional stake in a wider range of events, boosting viewing figures. This, of course, is exactly what sponsors seek.

The kind of Games I describe would involve most of civil society. Local government, schools and universities, all manner of community and voluntary groups, sporting, recreational and conservation organizations would all play a crucial part. Through this involvement the Five Rings symbol could be transformed. Instead of its widespread, legally guarded use by the sponsors, statutes would be passed to the opposite effect. Any commercial use of the Five Rings would be banned; only non-profit-making bodies would be permitted to use it in order to promote their involvement in, support for and association with the Games. The Five Rings would be recast as a badge of civic and sporting pride.

It will be objected that the Olympics need the money that corporations provide. But corporations need the Olympics too – negotiations should be much tougher. Selling off the Games to the highest bidder and in return meeting all demands to commercialize and commodify the Olympics isn't the only way to do business, nor is it necessarily good for each party. And while the interests of the sponsors are at present so jealously guarded, who is protecting the biggest sponsor of all – you and me, the taxpayers? A non-commercial Olympics doesn't mean one that can't be profitable – none of the New Rings are proposed with that aim in mind. The issue is how that profit is made and the effect it is allowed to have on the character of the Games. I envisage an Olympics in which the five rings stand for sport's values and are the sole and authorized property of sport and not of the sponsors.

My new Five Rings remain a symbol of the internationalism of the Olympics – that much stays the same. But they most certainly seek to stand for something else too. Each ring represents a value: decentralization; participation; sport for free; sport for all; sport as a value not a commodity. And all five are interlinked, with the happy consequence that the implementation of each bolsters the others. Five Rings, five colours, five links. No new Olympic symbol is required, just a new purpose behind it.

CHAPTER FOUR
Reimagining Olympism

The IOC claims in its 2008 *Global Television and Online Media Report* that 3.6 billion people, or 53% of the Earth's population, watched at least one minute of the action from the Beijing Games. Quite how such a statistic can be verified with any precision is unclear. Nevertheless, there's no doubt that the Games are one of the biggest shows on Earth.

In terms of attracting a global audience the Olympics have a number of advantages over football and other major sporting events. First, the Games have the longest history, predating football's first World Cup by almost 40 years, and the World Athletics Championship by just under a century. Second, there is no lengthy qualifying campaign to reduce the number of countries taking part to just 32 as is the case for the World Cup – practically every nation on the planet is represented at the Games. Some 205 national teams competed in Beijing; 216 are expected at London 2012. Third, unlike rival sporting attractions, the Olympics incorporate a wide range of different competitions: there will be 26 different sports on show in 2012. While, obviously, not all events are of equal interest around the world, together they offer something for everyone. Finally, despite the medal-winning positions in too many events being dominated by too few countries' athletes across the Games programme as a whole the... Olympic victors' podium is shared by an enormous diversity of medal winners. Competitors from Panama, the Dominican Republic and Estonia were among those collecting Gold in Beijing, while representatives of Mauritius, Moldova and Venezuela each picked up a Bronze. In the total 86 nations appeared in medals table at Beijing 2008, compared to just 39 at the 2011 World Athletics Championships.

The significance of the Olympics, however, extends beyond its history, range of participants and vast global reach. This occurred to me with particular force when, in the summer of 2005, I found myself on a tour of Berlin's *Olympiastadion*. Being an optimistic sort I'd decided to try to get a feel for the place where I fully anticipated England would be playing in the World Cup final twelve months later. I was of course disappointed in this expectation after England made their customary early exit, losing out in the quarterfinal to Portugal, following the misery of a penalty shootout. But my visit to the *Olympiastadion* turned out not to be a complete waste of time.

The stadium had been the main venue for the 1936 Olympics, forming part of the vast *Reichssportfeld*, the Nazi name for the Olympic Park, the construction of which was a pet project of Hitler's. Although, with typical German ingenuity it had been extensively rebuilt from the inside for the 2066 Word Cup finals. Much of the original outer structure which had survived Allied bombing and remained intact. As we completed our tour we were shown a stone plaque honouring those who had won medals in 1936. The name at the top of the list, with details of the four Golds he had won, was that of the black American runner Jesse Owens. Owens' victories had been an emphatic answer to the theories of racial supremacy propagated by Hitler and his followers. Accounts conflict as to whether the Führer stormed out of the stadium in a fit of anger as the American repeatedly defeated the finest specimens of Aryan athleticism that could be found. But one thing is certain: the most enduring story of the Nazi Games is, ironically, that medals are won by athletes, not races, master or otherwise. Despite the immense power of the Nazi leadership, Owens' name, chiselled into that plaque, was never removed and remains to this day a statement of hope and resistance. Just seeing it there made my visit entirely worthwhile and underscored the magical power of the Olympics to shake established orders.

My Five New Rings are an effort to engage with the Olympics and more especially with all those who share an emotional and physical attachment to sport, as fans or participants or both. But to do this requires not just the practical proposals I've advanced but something more. It needs a transformation of the ideology behind the Olympics, often referred to as Olympism, and the organization that embodies it, the IOC.

The version of the Olympic Charter adopted in 2011 opens with a noble-sounding definition:

'Olympism is a philosophy of life, exalting and combining in a balanced whole the qualities of body, will and mind. Blending sport with culture and education, Olympism seeks to create a way of life based on the joy of effort, the educational value of good example, social responsibility and respect for universal fundamental ethical principles.' It goes on to a list a number equally uplifting objectives: a harmonious, peaceful society, the practice of sport as a human right, the fight against discrimination. But after this promising start, the vast bulk of the document, a full 103 pages, is taken up with an instruction manual of how every Games should be organized. Symbols, mottos and emblems are all provided with strict image-rights protection. The role of the local organizing committee is rigidly circumscribed. Each host city is expected to follow the charter's diktats to the letter. The IOC's interests are treated throughout as paramount, with little or no concern for the cost to the host in terms of independence and expenditure. In this way the worthy values that frame Olympism are thwarted by

the interests of the very bureaucracy that is supposed to protect them. This is typical of a technocratic managerialism that
becomes all about delivery rather any original purpose.

As I neared the completion of this book I took a day off writing. In the morning I joined an Easter fun run; at lunchtime
was at the local pool with other parents looking on nervously as
our little ones learned to swim; I spent the afternoon watching
non-league Lewes FC, now under community ownership, battle their way to victory over Hastings United in the East Sussex
derby. All across Britain hundreds of thousands of people are
doing something similar every weekend and Bank Holiday. All
involved – players, coaches and managers, fundraisers, referees,
course marshals – engage in such activity out of a love for sport
and a commitment to their community. How can this vast
constituency in any way connect to a body like the IOC that
has more in common with a huge multinational big business
than a grassroots sports organization? Marketing, PR, sponsorship and event management are all important skills but they
should be used to serve sport, not run it. When these priorities
become reversed what is produced? A faceless, all-powerful,
self-perpetuating and self-interested clique. How many of us
know who serves on the IOC, how they are elected, to whom
they are accountable or what their responsibilities comprise?
Very few.

Finding ways to connect the IOC to grassroots sport should

be the first objective in reimagining Olympism. This is about more than simple reorganization. It entails a total change in Olympism's priorities. The World Health Organization (WHO) monitors and reports on health issues around the world, UNESCO defends the world's heritage sites, UNICEF speaks out for the world's children. The IOC needs to become a body more like these, one that focuses on the promotion of access to and participation in sport globally. And it needs to make this objective central to the organization of the Olympic Games.

In pursuing these objectives the IOC would have considerable leverage. Many critics have noted how the IOC has acquired powers and privileges that accord it the status of a quasi-state. This is because of the unique authority the IOC has in selecting host cities and appointing official sponsors. If changes in the IOC's priorities were linked to the bidding and sponsorship process the impact would be instant and considerable. No longer would cities compete on the basis of how grand were the facilities they promised to build, how dramatic was the backdrop they provided or how generous were the tax concessions they had on offer. Instead the bid would be assessed on the basis of their past achievement in levels of sports participation and access, the use-value of existing facilities, the proven record of support for sporting activities. To host the Games, bidders would be required first to prove that sport is accorded the priority it deserves in the range of overall social provision. Those cities and nations that were good for sport would be deemed to be good for the Games. The same principle would be applied to candidate sponsors: their corporate responsibility record in terms of proven support for participatory sport would be the critical factor rather than simply the scale of the deal on offer.

As construction work got underway at the Olympic Park my curiosity about what was taking shape steadily increased. The office of the company, Philosophy Football, I co-founded was at the time based on the third floor of a book distribution warehouse in Hackney Wick, and from there I had a panoramic view of the entire site. At one end of the development the stadium gradually emerged, big but nothing special compared to many in which I've watched international football around the world. In the far corner from my vantage point the Westfield Stratford City shopping centre sprouted. This always seemed a risky proposition, even more so with the onset of the recession. I regularly wondered at my window why, if a shopping centre really was the key to regenerating the East End of London, it was necessary to host the Olympics there at all. The West London Westfield seems to attract the shoppers without a stadium, velodrome and swimming pool in its backyard. At another end of the park I could just about see the unusual shape of the cycling velodrome, nicknamed 'the Pringle' in an unintended stroke of ambush marketing because of its roof design. Compared to the open green spaces of Victoria Park, just a javelin throw away on the other side of the A12, dual-carriageway the remainder of the park was occupied by so many office and other buildings that I could only foresee the area in the wake of 2012 resembling an up-market industrial estate. And despite having a business located just on its edge I wasn't seeing much evidence of the widely touted economic trickle-down in the area, unless you count the fast-food shops doing a bit better thanks to the passing trade of construction workers and the shiny new train station.

One building however did catch my eye as it emerged. The basketball arena was in the centre of my line of vision from our office. It is built in the purest white with a curious dimple effect on its outside walls. But its most unusual feature is that it's portable. That's right, a 12,000-seat fully enclosed stadium, big enough to stage the Olympic basketball matches, can be folded down and shipped wherever else in the world is hosting an event and in need of something similar. In the *Guardian* Jonathan Glancey described the potential of such an innovation:

'Imagine a future Olympics held in temporary and reusable buildings. Not only would this save cities from debt, redundant venues and white elephant awards, it would also mean that the Games could be held in those with precious little money to throw away. A low-cost travelling Olympics could tour the world.'

Glancey's article appeared in June 2011 just as I started work on this book. Part of my preparation as a writer is to obsessively cut out and keep pieces that might at some stage be of relevance to the argument forming in my mind. Jonathan's article went on to the 'legacy' pile and I was sure I'd use it at some stage. By Christmas 2011 I was already immersed in my research and as a bit of light relief I treated myself to some non-Olympic reading. *We Want Falmer* is the inspirational tale of the Brighton football fans who, for fifteen years, campaigned tirelessly for a ground to call their own. Denied a stadium, the club was forced to play for a considerable time at a converted athletics track, Withdean, with temporary stands. When I read that, at the end of each season, these seats were stripped down, packed on the back of a lorry and ended up providing the stands at the eighteenth hole of the British Open it reminded me again of the portable basketball arena.

Some months later, as I was finishing this book, Martyn Routledge, from the creative communications outfit Open Agency, emailed me with a brilliant idea to subvertise the official London 2012 branding. But the restrictions imposed by the Olympics are very severe. Just about every conceivable word and relevant image is legally protected, and plenty of noise has been made about the hefty fines to be imposed on anyone offending the IOC's copyright. Martyn's idea brilliantly circumvented the restrictions. It read simply: 'World Sports Day.

E20. This Year'. Nothing here was trademarked but the words effectively described the event, the place (the newly minted London postcode for Stratford Park) and the date. They also hinted at the level of sport most of us can realistically attain, the participative and accessible model that I have proposed for a better Games.

From the bottom of my cuttings pile I sought out the basketball arena piece. My imagination was now working in overdrive. In the 1990s, when concerns started to be raised about the mounting debts incurred by Olympic host cities stuck with facilities of no obvious continuing use, one idea was to give the Olympics a permanent site, with somewhere close to Mount Olympus in Greece being the most widely favoured contender. Nothing came of the proposal however and the fate of host cities and their unfulfilled promises rolled on. Martyn's subvertising idea with Jonathan's vision of a flat-pack Olympics together suggested to me something entirely different.

Imagine the IOC as not just a global guardian of access to and participation in sport but as a kind of giant global hire shop too – an enormous holding bay of fold-up arenas and stands full of seats, roll out AstroTurf pitches and other mobile playing surfaces, portable floodlights and even the Portaloos and signage that every Games needs. With a staff made up not of super high-paid bureaucrats but architects, civil engineers, landscape designers and event organizers, all trained to help facilitate the Games wherever they take place in a way that best suits the needs of the host. And why have just one host city, or even one host nation? Why not have a month of Olympic sport, taking place all over the world to include not only, the Paralympics, but also youth and veterans' Games too?

Imagine: a month of world sports days with the marathon in Addis Ababa; surfing on Bondi Beach, Australia; mountain biking in Orange County, California; the basketball in Chicago; taekwondo in Seoul; beach volleyball in Rio; judo in Tokyo; the football, yes please, in England. And these suggestions would just be for starters; over each quadrennial cycle new places would be found for each particular part of the Games. Imagine the greatest sporting event on earth as a thirty-day Olympiad held at sites across the planet in August once every four years. The whole world would not only watch together, but take part together too. Host Nation? The world. How long might it take – the 2024, 2028, 2032 Games maybe? That's my Olympic dream, and if I'm still around to see it happen I'll be first in the queue for tickets.

Not Just Running for Gold

It was in the summer of 1972 that I first started running. I was inspired not so much by the forthcoming Olympics, where my boyhood athletics hero Dave Bedford failed to win a medal, coming in a disappointing sixth in the 10,000 metres and, even further back, twelfth in the 5,000 metres. Instead I took up running as a kind of revenge mission against my PE teacher who throughout my first year at secondary school had subjected me to the weekly humiliation of singling me out for the classroom fatboy's head-start in the school cross-country race.

By the time I reached adulthood in the late 1970s those who, like me, ran long distances primarily for pleasure and physical self-satisfaction found ourselves renamed 'joggers'. We were part of a boom. In the USA the craze first began after Frank Shorter won the Munich 1972 Olympic Marathon. Road running had previously been even more unattractive to watch for the US TV audience than the interminable circuits of a

400-metre track that make up the 5,000m or 10,000m races. But Shorter's success, together with Jim Fixx's best-selling *Complete Book of Running*, helped popularize what was in effect a social movement of sport. Fun runs, charity runs, road races, all became part of a glorious explosion of physical activity just for the sake of keeping fit and having a good time. Participation was the aim, not winning. Fixx's book further boosted jogging's dynamic growth by setting out the case for regular exercise as the most effective antidote to the threat of heart trouble. The social movement was transforming itself into a fitness revolution.

As with so many cultural phenomena, what first began in the USA took off in the UK a few years later. Radio One DJ Jimmy Saville fronted a Sunday night BBC TV programme that aimed to persuade viewers of the virtues of long-distance running. Bedecked in Gold jewellery and puffing an occasional cigar, the middle-aged Saville was the opposite of what many would imagine a road runner to look like. But he regularly ran marathons to raise money for good causes, linking the very obvious joy he took from running to the benefits it could bring to others. Saville virtually invented the idea of the charity marathon runner and countless thousands followed his lead.

Evidence of running's increasing popularity was obvious with the first Sunday Times National Fun Run in 1978. Following a summer season of articles full of the virtues of physical fitness for the middle-aged and middle class, an astonishing 12,000 runners turned up. Three years later, in 1981, the first London Marathon took place. Organizer Chris Brasher, who won a Gold medal in the 3,000-metres teeplechase way back at the 1956 Melbourne Games, had heard of the growing popularity of mass-participation marathon running in the USA. Now aged 51, long past his peak as an elite runner but still physically fit, he went to New York both to write about the city's marathon and run it. His report in The *Observer* adopted a tone of missionary zeal:

> To believe this story you must believe that the human race can be one joyous family, working together, laughing together, achieving the impossible.
>
> I believe it because I saw it happen. Last Sunday, in one of the most trouble-stricken cities in the world, 11,532 men, women and children from 40 countries, assisted by over a million black, white and yellow people … laughed, cheered and suffered during the greatest folk festival the world has seen.… I wonder whether London could stage such a festival? We have the course, a magnificent course… But do we have the heart and the hospitality to welcome the world?

Over thirty years later the London Marathon has entered the public's sporting consciousness at the highest level, rivalling the FA Cup Final and the Derby as a truly 'national' event. The key to the appeal of this race, as well as the half-marathon or fun runs that take place in towns and cities across the country, is that anyone can take part, provided they have a minimum of stamina and commitment. Thus the Olympic Creed, first read out during the 1908 Games and a vital part of the ceremonial traditions at Games ever since, acquired some popular meaning: 'The most important thing in the Olympic Games is not to win but to take part'. When it comes to a marathon, everyone wins, merely by starting and finishing.

In the course of the 1980s running became an ever more socially acceptable activity. Seb Coe, Steve Ovett and Steve Cram fed the British public's appetite for international sporting glory, which in mid-1980s England was not being satisfied by the principle team sports. At cricket the empire struck back in 1984 with the humiliation of a 0-5 'whitewash' at the hands of the rampantly successful West Indies team. In the same year England's rugby team narrowly avoided the traditional 'wooden spoon' in the sport's Five Nations tournament, finishing second to last. And at football England had failed to qualify for the 1984 European Championships, as had all the other home nations.

But at the inaugural 1983 World Athletics Championships

Steve Cram won 1,500-metre Gold. A year later Coe won Olympic Gold at the same distance in Los Angeles, with Cram finishing second. Coe also picked up the Silver medal in the 800-metres. At those Games too Great Britain's Wendy Sly won Silver in the women's 3,000-metres. And Charlie Spedding, Britain's winner of the 1984 London Marathon followed this up with a Bronze medal in the Olympic Marathon, the first British medal in the event for 20 years.

The world supremacy of British middle-distance running is difficult to comprehend three decades on. Coe's 800m world record in 1981 was run in a time so fast that no one else could improve on it for sixteen years. Between 1979 and 1985 the 1,500-metres world record was held exclusively by British runners, apart from one month in 1983 when US athlete Sydney Maree spoilt our party. British runner Steve Jones added the Marathon world record in 1984, and in the Los Angeles Olympics' women's marathon Priscilla Welch, at 39 years old, finished a highly creditable sixth despite having only taken up the sport four years previously and being a heavy smoker until she did so.

Around a decade on, the mid-to-late-1990s was a period dubbed by Martin Jacques, my former editor at *Marxism Today*, as the 'Age of Sport'. Martin set out his argument in a piece for the *Observer* that I read after my customary Sunday morning run. Tony Blair had just achieved a landslide victory in the June

1997 election and, reading Martin's piece, I realized that sport was as good a way as any of explaining the shifts in society on which New Labour had capitalized. As Martin put it,

> The emergence of sport on to the wider stage has been intimately bound up with the breakdown of old compartments of class, age and gender. Sport has broken loose. In so doing its growth is interacting with and being driven by some of the most fundamental cultural trends of our times: the new aspirations of women, body and fitness, fashion, leisure and prosperity, the revolution in TV, the new values of business, globalisation. Sport is surfing all these trends and, in the process, being transformed by them. Sport defines the nature of our times: that is why it has become the metaphor of the Nineties.

Martin went on to catalogue those sports enjoying the most dynamic growth. He listed step aerobics, martial arts, mountain biking, squash, badminton, jogging, skateboarding, skiing, whitewater rafting, bungee jumping, weighttraining and rock climbing, identifying what that they all had in common: 'They are individual rather than team activities. While the traditional team games remain the great spectator sports, when it comes to participation there has been a dramatic shift in favour of individual activities. The age of individualism is reflected in the nature of the sporting activity we now pursue. The emphasis is on choice: differentiation, self-expression, creativity, fitness, health, the body.'

The optimistic tone of Martin's analysis was characteristic of the moment. After all, we'd just seen the back of eighteen years of Tory rule. For a generation that had grown up under the harsh strictures of Thatcherism we had every reason to be cheerful. But the consequences of these changes in sport proved to be a mixed blessing. It wasn't only post-Marxist commentators who had spotted such trends. The business end of sport's governing bodies, the new satellite-TV broadcasters and deregulated commercial radio stations, the newspaper proprietors, the major international sportswear manufacturers and high-street fashion chains, the corporate sponsors and advertisers and the executive hospitality companies – all sooner or later latched onto what was happening. Sport became transformed in the course of the next decade into something that was much more a commodity than it had ever been, a surface on which to stick an advertising logo, the means to boost TV ratings and sell newspapers, the route to untold riches for sportsmen and women at the elite level and for those who governed their sports too.

The commercialization of the Olympics was very much part of this process. At those first Games I can remember avidly watching, forty years ago Munich 72, US Athlete Dave Wottle had come from nowhere to win the 800 metres. A 2008 edition of the magazine *Running Times* carried a retrospective feature on Wottle's victory, describing it as "marking the end of the age of innocence for sport, for the Olympics." Wottle, newly married when the Games took place, would leave the Olympic Village for bouts of illicit post-nuptials between training sessions and heats. His pre-match nutrition consisted of Hershey's bars, a ritual based more on superstition (he had consumed the chocolate before winning races at his high school) than any scientifically determined benefit. These idiosyncrasies were notable enough, but what I remember Wottle for most was the battered golf cap he wore in every heat, including the final. He even wore this distinctive headgear on the winner's podium and forgot to take it off as the stars and stripes were run up the flagpole . He insisted that no disrespect was intended, still less an act of rebellion. He was, he claimed, simply distracted by the shock of an astonishing late charge from the back of the field that secured one of the greatest surprise Olympic victories of all time. At 600m, three quarters of the way through the race, he had been in last place. Racing from the back of the pack is a familiar tactic in middle-distance running but this was ridiculous. Incredibly, he grabbed victory by 0.3 seconds. It was an Olympic final few like me who watched it at the time are likely every to forget. But this innocence has seemed in the four decades since to evaporate as the gap between everyday participation in physical activity for pleasure and fun and professional elite sport has widened to an unbridgeable chasm. Sport has indeed become a metaphor for our age but mostly for the wrong reasons.

This transformation, however, has not stopped me running. I still try to get up before six each morning to set off on a run. Within minutes I'm out of the country town where I now live and my lungs and heart are pumping as I make it up the first hill of my ten-mile circuit. This opening stretch is a half-mile slog up the toughest of inclines but I hardly drop my pace, leaning into the hill. When I reach the top I generally still have the strength to accelerate over the final ridge, past the golf clubhouse, giving a wave to the groundsmen who are preparing the greens for the day's golfers. Now a slight gradient is in my favour but the surface is uneven so I try to concentrate on the path ahead, mindful that a trip or fall is always possible (last year I slipped and broke an arm). I shoo sheep and cattle out of my path and check my watch. Fifteen minutes have passed and I have covered two-and-a-bit miles, including that beast of a hill. I head on towards the summit and, having reached it, turn for home, picking up pace, looking to run faster on the way back. The final ascent is the first descent of half an hour earlier. This bugger used to be a climb that would turn my legs to jelly. Now I'm powering to the top, looking forward to the final three miles. I fairly sprint across the grass, before the big last hill down by the golf club. I'm always fearful when running downhill of gravity taking over, of losing control, of being unable to stop. I would never have made it as a fell runner. So I zigzag my way down, concentrating on keeping my grip. Finally I'm back on the flat of the town's pavements for the last stretch and an attempt at a finishing kick.

Generally I can cover the 10 miles in about 75 minutes. That's pretty good for my age but I'm not running to win anything. Neither am I trying to lose weight (there are more effective ways of doing that; in fact some physiologists point out that exercise can lead to overeating, which we justify to ourselves by the physical activity we have just undertaken). Nor do I do it primarily to keep well. The chances of heart disease are significantly reduced by regular running, it's true, but we joggers endure runner's knees and often lower immunity levels to colds and viruses. No, I run because it is a means of escape from the everyday, a valued hour or so when nothing much else intrudes or interferes. But there is something deeper going on as well.

Marx once wrote, 'All that is solid melts into air, all that is holy is profaned.' That is what the commercialization and commodifcation of sport threatens to do, to destroy its essential meaning as the pursuit of physical pleasure, individual or collective, and whatever perfection of the body we may be capable of aspiring to. It may be hopelessly romantic, I don't care, but as I ascend and descend the Sussex hills at the crack of dawn, a battered old pair of trainers on my feet, I can see myself as part of a popular movement of people who enjoy sport purely for fun and therefore are the antithesis of all that the Olympics has come to represent. I run free, for free. No rules, no sponsors, no entry fee, no national pride, nobody's stopwatch to calibrate the results except my own. I run because I can. This book is for us: for all who just do sport, whatever sport, in this simple cause of liberation.

Going the Extra Mile

If the argument in this book has sparked an interest in finding out more about the how and the why of sport as politics then a highly readable academic introduction to the subject is Garry Whannel's *Culture, Politics and Sport*. More journalistic accounts are provided by Simon Barnes' *The Meaning of Sport* and Ed Smith's *What Sport Tells Us about Life*.

In recent years there have been a whole range of excellent histories of the key Olympic Games. These seek to place the event in a broader social and cultural context yet at the same time provide a thrilling narrative of medals won or lost. *The First London Olympics 1908* by Rebecca Jenkins skilfully takes us back to the very beginnings of the modern Olympic Movement. Guy Walters' *Berlin Games: How Hitler Stole the Olympic Dream* details probably the most notorious Olympics of all. Janie Hampton's book on London's 1948 Games has a title some would say applies to 2012: *The Austerity Olympics*. It depicts a Games taking place just two years after the end of World War II. *Rome 1960* by David Maraniss captures a Games taking place as an arena of contest begins between another set of contenders, the USA and USSR in the Cold War. Eight years later another collision between American politics and the Olympics took place. This time it was Black Power, civil rights and race at an unforgettable medal ceremony. The story is told by one of the participants, John Carlos, in his autobiographical *The John Carlos Story*, co-written with Dave Zirin. *The 1972 Munich Olympics* by Kay Schiller and Christopher Young minutely unpicks almost every possible angle on these Games from the taking hostage of the Israeli athletes to the impact of the Olympics on West Germany–GDR relations.

The beautifully designed *The British Olympics: Britain's Olympic Heritage 1612–2012* by Martin Polley relates 2012 not only to its modern-era forerunners, 1948 and 1908, but also to an earlier Olympian British tradition of games. To go right back to the Games in Ancient Greece read Neil Faulkner's *A Visitor's Guide to the Ancient Greek Olympics*.

The 1980s and 1990s saw a critique of commerce and corruption in the Olympics in books written for a general audience. Amongst the first was *Five Ring Circus* edited by Alan Tomlinson and Garry Whannel, which came out ahead of the

1984 Olympics. A trilogy by investigative sports journalist Andrew Jennings, *The Lords of the Rings* (co-written with Vyv Simson), *The New Lords of the Rings* and *The Great Olympic Swindle*, covers mainly the Games from 1992 to 2000 but is rich in background material on the Olympics and the IOC that precedes this period.

A critical account of the Paralympics is provided by David Howe's pioneering work, *The Cultural Politics of the Paralympic Movement*.

For an entirely different kind of read, try possibly the only crime novel featuring an Olympic Games, Manuel Vázquez Montalbán's *An Olympic Death*, set in and around Barcelona '92.

Four films must be seen. *Chariots of Fire* is based on the 1924 Olympics. The controversial Leni Riefenstahl film of the 1936 Games, *Olympia*, gives an insight into the power and the evil of propaganda, however stylized. *Tokyo Olympiad*, Kon Ichikawa's film of the 1964 Games, mixes documentary and critique to stunning cinematic effect. And similarly Kevin Macdonald's *One Day in September* about the 1972 Games breaks with documentary film-making convention to provide a compelling account of the hostage-taking crisis the Munich Games will always be remembered for.

On the commercialisation of sport two particularly good books. Walter LaFeber's *Michael Jordan and the New Global*

Capitalism and Pitch Invasion : Adidas, Puma and the Making of Modern Sport by Barbara Smit..

For some broader political reading which helps explain the transformation of the Olympics I recommend two titles. *Get Real* by Eliane Glaser is a very good general book on the widening gap between staged appearances and the gritty reality that pervades corporate and political spin. The definitive critique of the rise and rise of brandculture and how this symbolizes the spread of a global corporate power which now dominates the Olympics remains Naomi Klein's *No Logo*. The best book I've read recently on race and national identity is Gary Younge's *Who Are We?*

The International Association of Sport Economists website can be found at www.iasecon.net. The Chelsea School, University of Brighton, where I am a research fellow, has a twitter feed which followers can use to keep up-to-date with the latest writings on sports culture, @sport_research.

Accounts of London as the 2012 Olympic host city from a variety of perspectives include Iain Sinclair's *Ghost Milk*, Bob Gilbert's *The Green London Way* and John Rees and Lindsey German's *A People's History of London*. The brilliant *OlymPics*, designed and published by Open Agency, depicts another Olympian London before the copyright-police start their patrols.

Slightly off-topic but with material of relevance to the claims of a London 2012 legacy is Anna Minton's *Ground Control*, a superb book on the privatization of public space. Another useful background read is Owen Hatherley's *A New Kind of Bleak*, which looks at the failure of urban regeneration, with a good insight into the Stratford project. Stephen Graham's *Cities Under Siege* again isn't specific to the Olympics but will help to develop an understanding of the significance and consequences of the Games' securitization programme.

How world champions are made, the conditions that determine success, is brilliantly covered in Matthew Syed's book *Bounce*.

A collection of critical Marxist approaches to sport is contained in *Marxism, Cultural Studies and Sport* edited by Ben Carrington and Ian McDonald. For an entirely oppositional view of global sport Marc Perelman's *Barbaric Sport* cannot be beaten.

An appreciation of the values of sport, how they developed historically and how they are both abided by and abused is provided by, Mihir Bose's *The Spirit of the Game*. On the future of the Olympic movement read *Post-Olympism* edited by John Bale and Mette Krogh Christensen.

Two of the best investigative sports journalists are David Conn and Dave Zirin. British-based Conn has a blog *Inside*

Sport, which can be found at www.guardian.co.uk/sport/david-conn-inside-sport-blog. Dave Zirin's website, mainly covering US sport, is at www.edgeofsports.com. For an authoritative critique of London 2012 and previous Games visit www.gamesmonitor.org.uk.

A number of websites from which campaigns of direct action against the Olympics will be organized exist including www.ourolympics.org and www.counterolympicsnetwork.wordpress.com. The Playfair initiative campaigns to expose the use of sweatshop labour in the manufacture of team Olympic kits and merchandizing, www.playfair2012.org.uk.

Alternatively, the official London 2012 website is www.london2012.com. The official website of the Olympic movement is www.olympics.org.

On the appeal and the simplicity of running read Richard Askwith's *Feet in the Clouds*, Haruki Murakami's *What I Talk about When I Talk about Running* and David Renton's *Lives; Running*. Two accounts of the conditions that create world-beating distance runners are Christopher McDougall's *Born to Run* and Adharanand Finn's *Running with the Kenyans*.

And finally for those who will be stuck in front of the TV watching every moment of the London 2012 action, read David Goldblatt and Johnny Acton's handbook *How To Watch the Olympics*, which usefully describes itself as 'an instant initiation to every sport'. And if my book hasn't exhausted your appetite for critical commentary on London 2012 add another to your bookshelf: John Sugden and Alan Tomlinson's collection of academic essays *Watching the Olympics*.